World Cup 2011

Manish Kumar

Vitasta

Vitasta Publishing Pvt. Ltd.
New Delhi

Published by
Renu Kaul Verma for
Vitasta Publishing Pvt. Ltd.
2/15, Ansari Road, Daryaganj,
New Delhi - 110 002

ISBN 978-93-80828-34-3

Layout by Vitasta Publishing Pvt. Ltd.
Printed by Vits Press, New Delhi

Publisher's Note

ICC World Cup generates tremendous amount of goodwill since nothing unites this country more than cricket. The game is played in every nook and corner of India irrespective of the literacy or availability of resources. It is an honour for any publisher and a great opportunity to bring a book on ICC cricket world cup to catch on the excitement.

We were overwhelmed with the response to our proposal from the trade and direct customers even before the book went to print. We have tried to make the book different that the ones available. Author Manish Kumar is a sports journalist and a cricket fan and we found him to be best person to do this job. We are impressed with the hard work he has put in to bring the book to shape.

The book was in fact the idea of our CEO Santosh Verma who located Manish and persuaded him to write the book at a short notice. After that they worked together in tandem. Santosh impressed with his untiring effort to ensure that the book was readers' friendly and readily available in the market. But for the nights he spent at the editorial, this book was not possible.

We could have generated more interest by putting photographs of cricketers on the cover but we wanted to keep the sanctity of the cup and hence we thought of putting the cup in the background of a cricketing ground. Manoj Kumar deserves full credit for putting our thoughts into action on the cover. The fire-ball signifies that those who hit the hardest will stay till the end.

Best Wishes

Author's Note

It's hard to ignore cricket, if or not your love for sports goes beyond being the average couch potato and proclaiming your nationalism by supporting your team on ESPN or TEN Sports!

There is something infectious about the game; it brings out a winning streak in every commoner like me, it's truly the most spectacular drama of all- with joy, jealousy, grief, hurt, victory, success and love.

Cricket to me, like most in this country is inspirational – the only place where I see a young man, with or without six packs, may or may not know how to dance, not exactly Brad Pitt's twin and yet beat the hell out of his adversary. The only place in the world, where normal men become superheroes within seconds… India to me is not a country obsessed with the sport, but a country with a vying motivation to dream… Cricket in a gamut of ways facilitates many of us to achieve our dreams!

The sport and I go back a long way (like pretty much everyone in this subcontinent!) –I remember my nana and nani visiting us at Tripura, my winter break in '77 and gifting my brother a 'SG' bat along with the red cherry. The bat and the ball became my object of affection ever since- study breaks, washroom breaks, tea breaks and even actual breaks, free time of any sort, used to be solely devoted to swinging the bat. Sometimes just in the air, at times in front of the mirror, sometimes with the bat my domestic help washed clothes from and most times just in my mind… Years later, my chatty 10-year-old daughter still suspects, me swinging the maid's bat buoyantly in the washroom, but so long as she has no evidence, the case is all mine!

In my growing up years I was quick to devour any book, I could lay my hands on about my cricketing idols - SMG (Sunil Manohar Gavaskar), Kapil Dev, Imran Khan and Sir Garfield Sobers. It also only helped that India's premier magazine, Sportsworld, was edited by one of my all-time favourite cricketers, MAK Pataudi.

It's for these reasons and many more that I didn't think twice before accepting my publishers' offer to pen a book on the 10th World Cup cricket. On second thought, also because I was born on the 10th. My generation was lucky to watch the 1983 World Cup live on TV – we in the north-east for a long time thought it was a conspiracy by Doordarshan to lose the link for the duration when the great Sir Issac Viv Richards started hammering the Indian attack, and eventually got out to a miracle of a catch pulled off by the legendary Kapil Dev. I'm yet to check out whether the blackout was national or specific to the remote north-east!

On a more serious note, I find it difficult to dismiss any cricketer. They are, after all, the best that the system has produced and represented their country in the best manner possible. Except probably Rajinder Goel, the great spinner who never got a chance to play for India despite taking 750 first-class wickets. My favourite all-time cricketers are (in the order they helped my team evolve): Tiger Pataudi, Sunny Gavaskar, Kapil Dev, Ravi Shastri, Sachin Tendulkar, Sourav Ganguly, Rahul Dravid and Virender Sehwag. For the longest, I also wanted India to patch up with Pakistan so that we could own all their bowlers from Sarfaraz Nawaz and Salim Jaffer to Imran Khan and Wasim Akram!

The 2011 World Cup is special for me and to the billions of Indians because we want our heroes to succeed – I want Tendulkar, Harbhajan and Sehwag (players in their 30s) to hang up their boots with a World Cup title. So that sitting in the couch when I join the ranks of septuagenarians I can win the debate that Tendulkar is indeed the best of all times!

I thank my publishers for supporting me from the very beginning, Santosh and Sudesh Verma and Renu Kaul – a big, big thank you to you all ! A special mention to Faiza for taking the rickshaw on early winter mornings from Jama Masjid just to unlock the office for an eccentric writer like me. To all the others who worked with me on this book and stayed up the long hours. And lastly, to my family without whose support I wouldn't have learnt to think, write or dream.

I take the responsibility for any error or mistake that may have cropped up inadvertently.

Manish Kumar
New Delhi

Venue Map

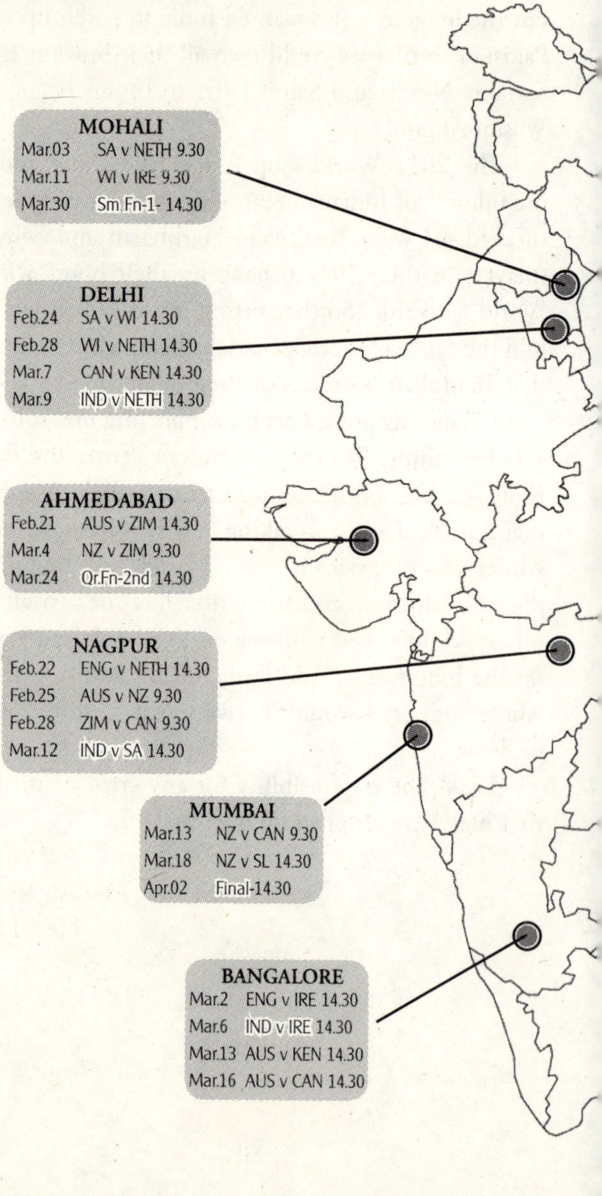
MOHALI
Mar.03 SA v NETH 9.30
Mar.11 WI v IRE 9.30
Mar.30 Sm.Fn-1- 14.30
DELHI
Feb.24 SA v WI 14.30
Feb.28 WI v NETH 14.30
Mar.7 CAN v KEN 14.30
Mar.9 IND v NETH 14.30
AHMEDABAD
Feb.21 AUS v ZIM 14.30
Mar.4 NZ v ZIM 9.30
Mar.24 Qr.Fn-2nd 14.30
NAGPUR
Feb.22 ENG v NETH 14.30
Feb.25 AUS v NZ 9.30
Feb.28 ZIM v CAN 9.30
Mar.12 IND v SA 14.30
MUMBAI
Mar.13 NZ v CAN 9.30
Mar.18 NZ v SL 14.30
Apr.02 Final-14.30
BANGALORE
Mar.2 ENG v IRE 14.30
Mar.6 IND v IRE 14.30
Mar.13 AUS v KEN 14.30
Mar.16 AUS v CAN 14.30

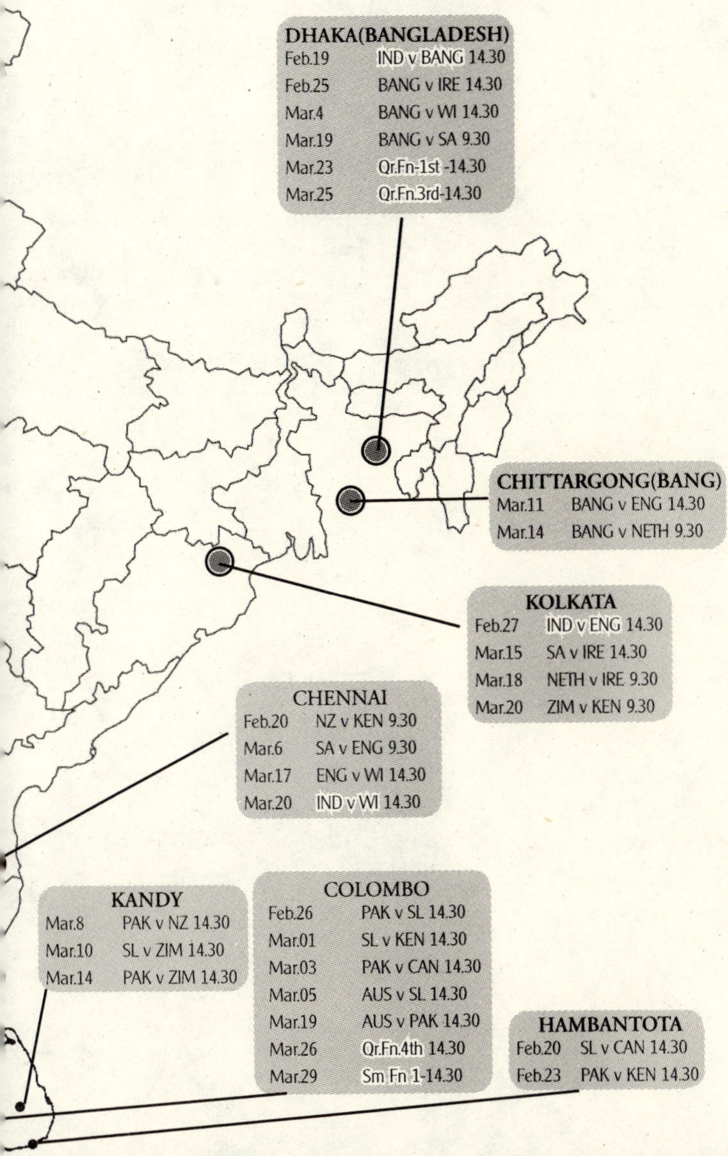
DHAKA(BANGLADESH)
Feb.19 IND v BANG 14.30
Feb.25 BANG v IRE 14.30
Mar.4 BANG v WI 14.30
Mar.19 BANG v SA 9.30
Mar.23 Qr.Fn-1st -14.30
Mar.25 Qr.Fn.3rd-14.30
CHITTARGONG(BANG)
Mar.11 BANG v ENG 14.30
Mar.14 BANG v NETH 9.30
KOLKATA
Feb.27 IND v ENG 14.30
Mar.15 SA v IRE 14.30
Mar.18 NETH v IRE 9.30
Mar.20 ZIM v KEN 9.30
CHENNAI
Feb.20 NZ v KEN 9.30
Mar.6 SA v ENG 9.30
Mar.17 ENG v WI 14.30
Mar.20 IND v WI 14.30
KANDY
Mar.8 PAK v NZ 14.30
Mar.10 SL v ZIM 14.30
Mar.14 PAK v ZIM 14.30
COLOMBO
Feb.26 PAK v SL 14.30
Mar.01 SL v KEN 14.30
Mar.03 PAK v CAN 14.30
Mar.05 AUS v SL 14.30
Mar.19 AUS v PAK 14.30
Mar.26 Qr.Fn.4th 14.30
Mar.29 Sm Fn 1-14.30
HAMBANTOTA
Feb.20 SL v CAN 14.30
Feb.23 PAK v KEN 14.30

Contents

History

(1975- 2007)

1975 World Cup

Carribean Calypso steals the show

There had been only 18 One-day Internationals (ODIs) played before the inaugural World Cup in 1975. Scepticism about the condensed version abounded in the run-up to the World Cup but once the "festival of cricket" got underway, the crowd thronged in thousands in most of the matches at the six venues, the world's finest cricketers took centre stage to produce some of the most scintillating knocks and stunning catches and runouts, and the rampaging West Indies skipper, Clive Lloyd, set up the victory for the favourites in a befitting climax—the five-day version had a big fight on hand.

Talking Points

- In the last-wicket huff and puff, Lillee hit a Van Holder no-ball straight to Fredericks at extra cover. The crowd missed the call and rushed on, thinking the match was over.
- In the first match of the World Cup, India crawled to 132/3 in 60 overs in response to England's 334/4. The biggest sore point was Sunil Gavaskar's knock of 36 not out, batting through the 60 overs.

The winner received £4000, the runners-up £2000 and the losing semifinalists £1000 each.

Stars

Clive Lloyd (WI)

The bespectacled caribbean skipper led his team of stars in exemplary style from the front and scored a brilliant ton in the finals. Talent-management was to become his forte after this victory.

Glenn Turner (NZ)

New Zealand had their captain to thank for taking them to the semifinals. When Turner clicked, his team won, when he didn't in two key matches they lost. The highest scorer, 333 runs.

Gary Gilmour (Aus)

Gilmour came as a late inclusion and only to feature in the semifinals and final. He reaped the highest haul of wickets in the WC, 11 wickets for just 62 runs in 24 overs.

The day of the final, June 21, was the longest day in the year. The match was played in front of a packed Lord's, approximately 26,000 people, and the last wicket tumbled at 8:41pm, as the West Indies completed victory by 17 runs over Australia after 118.4 overs. In an anti-climax Roy Fredericks trod on his wicket as he hooked Dennis Lillee out of the ground but the 'Big Cat' Lloyd took up the fight in memorable fashion, smashing 12 boundaries and two sixes in his 102, and the eventual 291 for 8 looked tough for Australia.

The drama was just building up – the early Australian batsmen lost out to the athletic fielding of Vivian Richards; and when the eventual looked simple, the fearsome duo of pacers Lillee and Jeff Thomson paired up for last-wicket partnership of 41runs, to produce the final twist. Inching close to an upset, however, the final run-out drove the last nail in their coffin. Such intense drama and incidents in one tournament, 15 matches held over a fortnight, a carnival atmosphere created by Carribean immigrants, the infamous English weather acting sporty for a change, the first World Cup silenced the skeptics.

Summary

Participating Teams: Australia, England, India, Pakistan, New Zealand, West Indies, East Africa and Sri Lanka (not a Test nation until 1982)

Format: Two qualifying groups of four, playing each other once in 60-over matches; top two in each group progressed to semi-finals; 15 matches in all

1st SF: England v Australia at Leeds - Jun 18; England 93 (36.2/60 ov); Australia 94/6 (28.4/60 ov) Australia won by 4 wickets

2nd SF: New Zealand v West Indies at The Oval on Jun 18; New Zealand 158 (52.2/60 ov); West Indies 159/5 (40.1/60 ov). West Indies won by five wickets

> “Pig’s arse... We’ve been running up and down here all afternoon”
>
> – Jeff Thomson, on the incidents during his last wicket partnership with Dennis Lillee in the final

Final: Australia v West Indies at Lord’s - Jun 21, 1975; West Indies 291/8 (60/60 ov); Australia 274 (58.4/60 ov); West Indies won by 17 runs

Player of the match CH Lloyd (West Indies)
Umpires HD Bird and TW Spencer

Twenty-six thousand people watched the final at the Lord’s where the gate receipt were £66,000, then a record for an ODI.

Scorecard - Final

West Indies innings (60 overs maximum)		R	M	B	4s	6s	SR
RC Fredericks	hit wicket b Lillee	7	14	13	0	0	53.84
CG Greenidge	c †Marsh b Thomson	13	80	61	1	0	21.31
AI Kallicharran	c †Marsh b Gilmour	12	26	18	2	0	66.66
RB Kanhai	b Gilmour	55	156	105	8	0	52.38
CH Lloyd*	c †Marsh b Gilmour	102	108	85	12	2	120.00
IVA Richards	b Gilmour	5	12	11	1	0	45.45
KD Boyce	c GS Chappell b Thomson	34	43	37	3	0	91.89
BD Julien	not out	26	54	37	1	0	70.27
DL Murray†	c & b Gilmour	14	11	10	1	1	140.00
VA Holder	not out	6	1	2	1	0	300.00
Extras	(lb 6, nb 11)	17					
Total	(8 wickets; 60 overs)	291	(4.85 runs per over)				

Did not bat AME Roberts

Fall of wickets 1-12 (Fredericks), 2-27 (Kallicharran), 3-50 (Greenidge), 4-199 (Lloyd), 5-206 (Kanhai), 6-209 (Richards),7-261 (Boyce), 8-285 (Murray)

Bowling	O	M	R	W	Econ
DK Lillee	12	1	55	1	4.58
GJ Gilmour	12	2	48	5	4.00
JR Thomson	12	1	44	2	3.66
MHN Walker	12	1	71	0	5.91
GS Chappell	7	0	33	0	4.71
KD Walters	5	0	23	0	4.60

Australia innings (target: 292 runs from 60 overs)		R	M	B	4s	6s	SR
A Turner	run out (Richards)	40	85	54	4	0	74.07
RB McCosker	c Kallicharran b Boyce	7	29	24	1	0	29.16
IM Chappell*	run out (Richards/Lloyd)	62	125	93	6	0	66.66
GS Chappell	run out (Richards)	15	24	23	2	0	65.21
KD Walters	b Lloyd	35	52	51	5	0	68.62
RW Marsh†	b Boyce	11	34	24	0	0	45.83
R Edwards	c Fredericks b Boyce	28	51	37	2	0	75.67
GJ Gilmour	c Kanhai b Boyce	14	16	11	2	0	127.27
MHN Walker	run out (Holder)	7	10	9	1	0	77.77
JR Thomson	run out (†Murray)	21	32	21	2	0	100.00
DK Lillee	not out	16	29	19	1	0	84.21
Extras	(b 2, lb 9, nb 7)	18					
Total	(all out; 58.4 overs)	274	(4.67 runs per over)				

Fall of wickets 1-25 (McCosker), 2-81 (Turner), 3-115 (GS Chappell), 4-162 (IM Chappell), 5-170 (Walters), 6-195 (Marsh),7-221 (Gilmour), 8-231 (Edwards), 9-233 (Walker), 10-274 (Thomson)

Bowling	**O**	**M**	**R**	**W**	**Econ**
BD Julien	12	0	58	0	4.83
AME Roberts	11	1	45	0	4.09
KD Boyce	12	0	50	4	4.16
VA Holder	11.4	1	65	0	5.57
CH Lloyd	12	1	38	1	3.16

1979 World Cup

Double joy for West Indies

West Indies' domination of the game was in full display at the 1979 edition. As expected, they made their progress in a ruthless fashion and their pyrotechnics were in full flow against England in the final. It turned out to be one of the most lop-sided contests at this level in the history of the game.

Talking Points

- In the final, centurion Vivian Richards ended his and the West Indian innings in style by walking across the stumps and flicking Hendrick into the Mound Stand for a huge six.
- Geoff Boycott turned out to be England's unlikely bowling secret weapon, his little medium-pacers snaring two for 15 vs Aus, and two for 14 at the death against Pakistan.

This was the World Cup where one of the all-time greats Vivian Richards rode the pitch like a colossus. While his athletic fielding in the final of the 1975 edition paved the way for their maiden title, this time Richards played the destroyer with both the ball and bat, against Pakistan in the semifinals and England in the finals respectively.

On the backfoot at 99 for four wickets in the

The minor teams emerged from a qualifying competition, the inaugural ICC Trophy, which was won by Sri Lanka

Stars

Vivian Richards (WI)

The 'King' demolished England in one of the most memorable knocks ever seen. More than the quality of the English attack, it was the merciless thrashing which contributed to the aura of Richards.

Fearsome quartet (WI)

Colin Croft-Andy Roberts-Mike Holding-Joel Garner forged one of the most formidable battery of bowlers in the history of ODIs, each of them grabbing eight wickets apiece, to make a handsome contribution.

Mike Hendrick (Eng)

The Englishman emerged the highest wicket-taker in the tournament. Though Hendrick was at the receiving end in the final, he grabbed 10 wickets at the cost of 149 runs in five matches.

final, the defending champions cut loose as Richards (unbeaten 138 off 157 balls, three 6s, 11 4s) and Collis King (86 runs off 66 balls) blasted the English attack to set up 286 for nine. Arguably, the defining moment was Richards ending the innings by walking across his stumps and flicking Hendrick into the Mound Stand for six. England started cautiously but too slowly, putting on 129 runs for the opening stand after exhausting more than the halfway of the total overs. Joel Garner who had recently joined the Caribbean battery of quickies, scalped five wickets for just 38 runs to squash the English challenge. From 183 for two, England were dismissed for 194, to give West Indies their World Cup title No 2 in a row.

Pakistan made their entry into the semifinal for the first time while Australia fielded an unknown team, having lost a number of their stars to the Kerry Packer series. India suffered a shocking defeat at the hands of Sri Lanka. Kapil Dev made his debut. Little did he or India know that four years hence he would be holding the trophy in his hand.

Summary

Participating Teams: Australia, England, India, Pakistan, New Zealand, West Indies, Canada and Sri Lanka (not a Test nation until 1982)

Format: Two qualifying groups of four, playing each other once in 60-over matches; top two in each group progressed to semi-finals; 15 matches in all.

1st SF: Eng v NZ at Manchester on Jun 20. Eng 221/8 (60 ov); NZ 212/9 (60 ov). Eng won by 9 runs.

2nd SF: Pak v WI at The Oval on Jun 20. WI 293/6 (60 ov); Pak 250 (56.2 ov). WI won by 43 runs.

> "The 1979 World Cup victory was one which I felt meant even more than usual for West Indies cricket"
>
> —Clive Lloyd

Final: England v West Indies at Lord's on Jun 23. WI 286/9 (60 ov); England 194 (51 ov). West Indies won by 92 runs.

Player of the match IVA Richards (West Indies)
Umpires HD Bird and BJ Meyer

West Indies and Pakistan, fearing a backlash at home if they performed badly, chose all their World Series Cricket players

Scorecard - Final

West Indies innings (60 overs maximum)		**R**	**M**	**B**	**4s**	**6s**	**SR**
CG Greenidge	run out (Randall)	9	31	31	0	0	29.03
DL Haynes	c Hendrick b Old	20	49	27	3	0	74.07
IVA Richards	not out	138	207	157	11	3	87.89
AI Kallicharran	b Hendrick	4	19	17	0	0	23.52
CH Lloyd*	c & b Old	13	42	33	2	0	39.39
CL King	c Randall b Edmonds	86	77	66	10	3	130.30
DL Murray†	c Gower b Edmonds	5	12	9	1	0	55.55
AME Roberts	c Brearley b Hendrick	0	8	7	0	0	0.00
J Garner	c †Taylor b Botham	0	4	5	0	0	0.00
MA Holding	b Botham	0	7	6	0	0	0.00
CEH Croft	not out	0	6	2	0	0	0.00
Extras	(b 1, lb 10)	11					
Total	(9 wickets; 60 overs)	286	(4.76 runs per over)				

Fall of wickets 1-22 (Greenidge), 2-36 (Haynes), 3-55 (Kallicharran), 4-99 (Lloyd), 5-238 (King), 6-252 (Murray),7-258 (Roberts), 8-260 (Garner), 9-272 (Holding)

Bowling	**O**	**M**	**R**	**W**	**Econ**
IT Botham	12	2	44	2	3.66
M Hendrick	12	2	50	2	4.16
CM Old	12	0	55	2	4.58
G Boycott	6	0	38	0	6.33
PH Edmonds	12	2	40	2	3.33
GA Gooch	4	0	27	0	6.75
W Larkins	2	0	21	0	10.50

England innings (target: 287 runs from 60 overs)		**R**	**M**	**B**	**4s**	**6s**	**SR**
JM Brearley*	c King b Holding	64	130	130	7	0	49.23
G Boycott	c Kallicharran b Holding	57	137	105	3	0	54.28
DW Randall	b Croft	15	36	22	0	0	68.18
GA Gooch	b Garner	32	31	28	4	0	114.28
DI Gower	b Garner	0	6	4	0	0	0.00
IT Botham	c Richards b Croft	4	7	3	0	0	133.33
W Larkins	b Garner	0	1	1	0	0	0.00
PH Edmonds	not out	5	14	8	0	0	62.50
CM Old	b Garner	0	4	2	0	0	0.00
RW Taylor†	c †Murray b Garner	0	1	1	0	0	0.00
M Hendrick	b Croft	0	4	5	0	0	0.00
Extras	(lb 12, w 2, nb 3)	17					
Total	(all out; 51 overs)	194	(3.80 runs per over)				

Fall of wickets 1-129 (Brearley), 2-135 (Boycott), 3-183 (Gooch), 4-183 (Gower), 5-186 (Randall), 6-186 (Larkins),7-192 (Botham), 8-192 (Old), 9-194 (Taylor), 10-194 (Hendrick)

Bowling	**O**	**M**	**R**	**W**	**Econ**
AME Roberts	9	2	33	0	3.66
MA Holding	8	1	16	2	2.00
CEH Croft	10	1	42	3	4.20
J Garner	11	0	38	5	3.45
IVA Richards	10	0	35	0	3.50
CL King	3	0	13	0	4.33

1983 World Cup

Kapil's Devils stun the world

It's probably the most enshrined visual that India remembers after August 15, 1947. In hind sight it also seems to mark the day when the World Cup became unfettered from the tag of favourites. India stunned the world on that fateful June 25, 1983, and since then a sequence of World Cups became an open tournament. Australia in 1987, Pakistan in 1992 and Sri Lanka in 1996, have used the stage to show what the underdog can achieve.

Talking Points

- Coming in to bat against Zimbabwe at 17/5, Kapil Dev blasted an undefeated 175 out of the team's total of 266/8, with 16 fours and six sixes, for India's stunning 31-run win
- Krish Srikkanth hooking the fearsome Andy Robert for a six into the lower tier of the Warner Stand in the final, this after the English commentator remark that the bowler was 'setting him up'

Nobody, least of all the pundits and punters, percieved India as a potential champion. It is only now when one looks back the component of the Kapil's team - a gritty middle-order, a number of all-rounders, the wily mix of gentle pace and spin in the bowling attack

In Kapil Dev's 175, including 16 fours and six sixes, he put on a Cup-record 126 for the ninth wicket with Syed Kirmani.

Stars

Kapil Dev (Ind)

For his astute captaincy at just 24, explosive batting against Zimbabwe that rescued his team from death, the skier off Viv Richards that he grabbed out of nowhere to turn the final on its head.

Mohinder Amarnath(Ind)

The son of one of the grittiest Indian cricketers to have played the game, Mohinder rose to the occasion with his great all-round performance and was the best player of the 1983 World Cup

Roger Binny (Ind)

Another indefatigable all-rounder who emerged the highest wicket-taker of the tournament, with a series winning effort of 18 wickets, at an impressive average of 18.66 from eight matches.

and the attacking Krish Srikkanth, that the World Cup victory seems to fall in place.

India started their campaign on a winning note, beating West Indies, surviving a scare from Zimbabwe, sailing past Australia, and beating England in the semifinal to set up a final against the two-time champions. India made 183 after being put to bat, and that low score turned out to be a winning one as West Indies collapsed for 140, one of the greatest upsets in the history of the sport.

Sandhu provided the much-needed breakthrough, dismissing opener Greenidge. The turning point was the dismissal of Richards, who batting on 33 from 27 balls, tried pulling Madan Lal but the shot didn't clear the field. Instead, the ball rose higher and higher and Kapil Dev who had to run several metres, caught the ball awkwardly. The West Indies' batting swung like a pendulum–from 50 for one they were reduced to 66 for five, and it was just a matter of a few overs before Kapil's Devils changed the cricket order.

Summary

Participating Teams: Australia, England, India, Pakistan, New Zealand, West Indies, Sri Lanka and Zimbabwe

Format: Two groups of four, each team played the others in its group twice, to determine the four semifinalists. The idea was to reduce the chances of elimination by the weather. For the first time, non-Test grounds were used.

1st SF: England v India at Manchester–Jun 22; England 213 (60/60 ov); India 217/4 (54.4/60 ov); India won by six wickets

2nd SF: Pakistan v West Indies at The Oval–Jun 22; Pakistan 184/8 (60/60 ov); West Indies 188/2 (48.4/60 ov); Windies won by 8 wickets

"It was Kapil Dev's mad captaincy that won us the World Cup. To be honest, there was no hope of going beyond the group stages"

– Krish Srikkanth

Final: India v West Indies at Lord's–Jun 25; India 183 (54.4/60 ov); West Indies 140 (52 ov). India won by 43 runs

Player of the match M Amarnath (India)
Umpires HD Bird and BJ Meyer

Madan Lal and Mohinder Amarnath grabbed three wickets each in the final to dismiss the West Indies for 140

Scorecard - Final

India innings (60 overs maximum)		R	M	B	4s	6s	SR
SM Gavaskar	c †Dujon b Roberts	2	14	12	0	0	16.66
K Srikkanth	lbw b Marshall	38	82	57	7	1	66.66
M Amarnath	b Holding	26	108	80	3	0	32.50
Yashpal Sharma	c sub (AL Logie) b Gomes	11	45	32	1	0	34.37
SM Patil	c Gomes b Garner	27	48	29	0	1	93.10
N Kapil Dev*	c Holding b Gomes	15	10	8	3	0	187.50
KBJ Azad	c Garner b Roberts	0	3	3	0	0	0.00
RMH Binny	c Garner b Roberts	2	9	8	0	0	25.00
S Madan Lal	b Marshall	17	31	27	0	1	62.96
SMH Kirmani†	b Holding	14	55	43	0	0	32.55
BS Sandhu	not out	11	42	30	1	0	36.66
Extras	(b 5, lb 5, w 9, nb 1)	20					
Total	(all out; 54.4 overs)	183	(3.34 runs per over)				

Fall of wickets 1-2 (Gavaskar), 2-59 (Srikkanth), 3-90 (Amarnath), 4-92 (Yashpal Sharma), 5-110 (Kapil Dev), 6-111 (Azad), 7-130 (Binny), 8-153 (Patil), 9-161 (Madan Lal), 10-183 (Kirmani)

Bowling	**O**	**M**	**R**	**W**	**Econ**
AME Roberts	10	3	32	3	3.20
J Garner	12	4	24	1	2.00
MD Marshall	11	1	24	2	2.18
MA Holding	9.4	2	26	2	2.68
HA Gomes	11	1	49	2	4.45
IVA Richards	1	0	8	0	8.00

West Indies innings (target: 184 runs from 60 overs)		R	M	B	4s	6s	SR
CG Greenidge	b Sandhu	1	11	12	0	0	8.33
DL Haynes	c Binny b Madan Lal	13	45	33	2	0	39.39
IVA Richards	c Kapil Dev b Madan Lal	33	42	28	7	0	117.85
CH Lloyd*	c Kapil Dev b Binny	8	32	17	1	0	47.05
HA Gomes	c Gavaskar b Madan Lal	5	18	16	0	0	31.25
SFAF Bacchus	c †Kirmani b Sandhu	8	37	25	0	0	32.00
PJL Dujon†	b Amarnath	25	94	73	0	1	34.24
MD Marshall	c Gavaskar b Amarnath	18	73	51	0	0	35.29
AME Roberts	lbw b Kapil Dev	4	16	14	0	0	28.57
J Garner	not out	5	34	19	0	0	26.31
MA Holding	lbw b Amarnath	6	28	24	0	0	25.00
Extras	(lb 4, w 10)	14					
Total	(all out; 52 overs)	140	(2.69 runs per over)				

Fall of wickets 1-5 (Greenidge), 2-50 (Haynes), 3-57 (Richards), 4-66 (Gomes), 5-66 (Lloyd), 6-76 (Bacchus), 7-119 (Dujon), 8-124 (Marshall), 9-126 (Roberts), 10-140 (Holding)

Bowling	**O**	**M**	**R**	**W**	**Econ**
N Kapil Dev	11	4	21	1	1.90
BS Sandhu	9	1	32	2	3.55
S Madan Lal	12	2	31	3	2.58
RMH Binny	10	1	23	1	2.30
M Amarnath	7	0	12	3	1.71
KBJ Azad	3	0	7	0	2.33

1987 World Cup

The Oz Magic at the Eden

The first World Cup to be staged outside England had obviously many new additions and firsts. Holding the tournament in the subcontinent also marked a fresh attempt through the sport to forge friendship between arch-rivals India and Pakistan. The sub-continental edition was widely watched, intensely contested, more vibrant than the previous World Cups, had more venues and involved more travelling for the teams. It was also the first to feature spinning tracks and neutral umpires.

Talking Points

- The Little Master, Sunil Gavaskar, having hit his first and only ODI century against New Zealand, made his last international appearance in Mumbai, at his home ground
- India's Chetan Sharma made first hat-trick in the history of the tournament when he clean bowled Ken Rutherford, Ian Smith and Ewen Chatfield of New Zealand off consecutive balls

The eventual result also marked the beginning of Australia's domination. The host teams' script went awry in the semifinals–Graham Gooch and Mike Gatting swept aside India's aspiration for a double title

19 out of 27 matches were won by the side batting first, so most teams wanted to bowl first and determine the target.

Stars

Allan Border (Aus)

Captaincy played a major role for the winning team once again. Border lifted the spirits of his team when they were in the dumps, with Zaheer Abbas dismissing them as a bunch of county club players

Craig McDermott (Aus)

The World Cup was played on spinning track but the highest wicket-taker was a fast bowlers. McDermott equalled the WC record of 18 wickets and rose to the occasion in the final

David Houghton (Zim)

Here was a batsman from the minnows who could take the battle into the rival camp. The batsman with the golden locks went berserk against New Zealand, scoring a brilliant 142

while Steve Waugh (18 off the final over) and Craig McDermott (5/54) slammed the doors on Pakistan.

The oldest rivalry in cricket was re-enacted in a grand setting; England and Australia reached the final held at the Eden Gardens. Australia won the toss and, like most teams in the tournament, chose to bat first. They were off to a flying start with GR Marsh and DC Boon amassing 52 runs in the first 10 overs. The runs flowed as Boon topscored with 75 and Australia closed at 253 for five in 50 overs.

Gooch and Gatting responded in similar fashion as they did against India in the semis till the latter's reverse-sweep took the top edge, bounced off his shoulder, and was snapped up by Greg Dyer behind the wickets. England struggled without their skipper, and kept on tight lease in the final over by McDermott as Australia scampered home by seven runs.

Summary

Teams: Australia, England, India, New Zealand, Pakistan, Sri Lanka, West Indies, Zimbabwe

Format: Same as 1983. However, due to the shorter daylight hours on the subcontinent, matches were 50 overs per innings, not 60. A third-place playoff between Pakistan and India was to be staged keeping in mind the disappointment of the local crowd, but the star players demanded too much cash.

1st SF: Pakistan v Australia at Lahore - Nov 4, 1987
Aus 267/8 (50 ov); Pak 249 (49 ov). Australia won by 18 runs.

2nd SF: India v England at Mumbai – Nov 5, 1987. England 254/6 (50 ov); India 219 (45.3 ov). England won by 35 runs.

"When I look back at the title, it was probably the turnaround and the start of better times for us"

—Allan Border

Final: Australia v England at Kolkata – Nov 8, 1987
Australia 253/5 (50 ov); England 246/8 (50 ov)
Australia won by 7 runs.

Player of the match DC Boon (Australia)
Umpires RB Gupta and Mahboob Shah (Pakistan)

West Indies failed to reach the semifinals for the first time, despite their 191-run annihilation of Sri Lanka

Scorecard - Final

Australia innings (50 overs maximum)		**R**	**M**	**B**	**4s**	**6s**	**SR**
DC Boon	c †Downton b Hemmings	75	159	125	7	0	60.00
GR Marsh	b Foster	24	71	49	3	0	48.97
DM Jones	c Athey b Hemmings	33	75	57	1	1	57.89
CJ McDermott	b Gooch	14	6	8	2	0	175.00
AR Border*	run out (Robinson/ †Downton)	31	48	31	3	0	100.00
MRJ Veletta	not out	45	50	31	6	0	145.16
SR Waugh	not out	5	5	4	0	0	125.00
Extras	(b 1, lb 13, w 5, nb 7)	26					
Total	(5 wickets; 50 overs)	253	(5.06 runs per over)				

Fall of wickets 1-75 (Marsh), 2-151 (Jones), 3-166 (McDermott), 4-168 (Boon), 5-241 (Border)

Bowling	**O**	**M**	**R**	**W**	**Econ**
PAJ DeFreitas	6	1	34	0	5.66
GC Small	6	0	33	0	5.50
NA Foster	10	0	38	1	3.80
EE Hemmings	10	1	48	2	4.80
JE Emburey	10	0	44	0	4.40
GA Gooch	8	1	42	1	5.25

England innings (target: 254 runs from 50 overs)		R	M	B	4s	6s	SR
GA Gooch	lbw b O'Donnell	35	74	57	4	0	61.40
RT Robinson	lbw b McDermott	0	2	1	0	0	0.00
CWJ Athey	run out (Waugh/Reid)	58	126	103	2	0	56.31
MW Gatting*	c †Dyer b Border	41	55	45	3	1	91.11
AJ Lamb	b Waugh	45	56	55	4	0	81.81
PR Downton†	c O'Donnell b Border	9	13	8	1	0	112.50
JE Emburey	run out (Boon/McDermott)	10	27	16	0	0	62.50
PAJ DeFreitas	c Reid b Waugh	17	10	10	2	1	170.00
NA Foster	not out	7	12	6	0	0	116.66
GC Small	not out	3	6	3	0	0	100.00
Extras	(b 1, lb 14, w 2, nb 4)	21					
Total	(8 wickets; 50 overs)	246	(4.92 runs per over)				

Fall of wickets 1-1 (Robinson), 2-66 (Gooch), 3-135 (Gatting), 4-170 (Athey), 5-188 (Downton), 6-218 (Emburey),7-220 (Lamb), 8-235 (DeFreitas)

Bowling	**O**	**M**	**R**	**W**	**Econ**
CJ McDermott	10	1	51	1	5.10
BA Reid	10	0	43	0	4.30
SR Waugh	9	0	37	2	4.11
SP O'Donnell	10	1	35	1	3.50
TBA May	4	0	27	0	6.75
AR Border	7	0	38	2	5.42

1992 World Cup

Imran's Tigers Turn the Corner

Cricket's most mercurial team finally found its calling in a country which is known to approach the game in an irreverent manner, least of all popularizing coloured clothing and floodlight matches. Pakistan, unlucky not to reach the final even once, was plucky in the early stage of the tournament co-hosted by Australia and New Zealand, somehow survived the rain-marred match against England, and miraculously lifted themselves under the inspiring Imran Khan to win the crown. Post-Independence, the subcontinent was finally looking happy with equal distribution of the prize that came from inheriting the colonial game —India won the Cup in 1983 and Pakistan nine years hence.

Talking Points

- New Zealand captain Martin Crowe used two innovative tactics – opened his team's bowling with a spin bowler, Dipak Patel, and opened the batting with "pinch hitters", such as Mark Greatbatch
- The 1992 World Cup was the first to feature coloured player clothing, white cricket balls and black sightscreens with a number of matches being played under floodlights

South Africa was allowed to re-join the ICC after the end of apartheid, and played their first World Cup in 1992

Stars

Wasim Akram (Pak)

The left arm quickie was in lethal form and demolished the English middle order to set up his team's victory in the final. No surprise that Akram emerged as the highest wicket-taker in the tournament with a haul of 18 wickets

Inzamam-ul-Haq(Pak)

The burly Pakistani batsman played a crucial role in the final and the only match against New Zealand. Inzy was the toast of his captain Imran Khan who stopped at nothing to boost his confidence

Martin Crowe (NZ)

The Kiwi skipper proved to be an astute leader and made two major innovations, including using pinch hitter Mark Greatbatch to great effect. Crowe was also the highest scorer (456 runs) of the tournament

It was Pakistan vs England in the final and the former looked completely determined to inscribe their name on the Cup. Their two stalwarts, Javed Miandad (scored 58 batting with a runner) and Imran Khan (72 runs) slowly resurrecting the innings with a 139-run partnership after Derek Pringle had dismissed their openers at 24. Late flourishes from Inzamam-ul-haq (42 off 35 balls) and Wasim Akram (33 off 18 balls) took Pakistan to a fighting total of 249 for six.

England had a shaky start, and lost four wickets for just 69 runs. Akram returned to change the course of the match for Pakistan–his two consecutive magical deliveries got rid of the solid Lamb and the dangerous Chris Lewis. In the end, Pakistan lifted the Cup, beating England by 22 runs.

The Indian angle was short and swift, they never looked confident to progress beyond the round robin. South Africa returned to the fold in great style, beating Australia in their opener. They were unfortunate to lose the semifinals to England in ludicrous circumstances when, after a rain delay, their revised target was set to score an impossible 21 runs from one ball.

Summary

Participating Teams: Australia, England, India, New Zealand, Pakistan, South Africa, Sri Lanka, West Indies and Zimbabwe

Format: It was changed from previous tournaments in that a complete round robin replaced the use of two qualifying groups. South Africa was the ninth team in the lot. The rule for calculating the target score for the team batting second in rain-affected matches was also changed.

1st SF: NZ v Pak at Auckland – March 21, 1992; New Zealand 262/7 (50 ov); Pakistan 264/6 (49 ov); Pakistan won by four wickets.

> "I attacked with all the available weapons. We used to sit for hours and do our planning"
>
> – Imran Khan, Pakistan captain

2nd SF: England v South Africa at Sydney –Mar 22, 1992. England 252/6 (45/45 ov); South Africa 232/6 (43/43 ov); England won by 19 runs.

Final: England v Pakistan at Melbourne–Mar 25, 1992. Pakistan 249/6 (50 ov); England 227 (49.2 ov). Pakistan won by 22 runs.

Player of the match Wasim Akram (Pakistan)
Umpires BL Aldridge (NZ) and SA Bucknor (WI)

A contest between all-round great Ian Botham and master blaster Sachin Tendulkar ended in favour of the former

Scorecard - Final

Pakistan innings (50 overs maximum)		**R**	**M**	**B**	**4s**	**6s**	**SR**
Aamer Sohail	c †Stewart b Pringle	4	20	19	0	0	21.05
Rameez Raja	lbw b Pringle	8	36	26	1	0	30.76
Imran Khan*	c Illingworth b Botham	72	159	110	5	1	65.45
Javed Miandad	c Botham b Illingworth	58	125	98	4	0	59.18
Inzamam-ul-Haq	b Pringle	42	46	35	4	0	120.00
Wasim Akram	run out (†Stewart)	33	21	18	4	0	183.33
Saleem Malik	not out	0	2	1	0	0	0.00
Extras	(lb 19, w 6, nb 7)	32					
Total	(6 wickets; 50 overs)	249	(4.98 runs per over)				

Fall of wickets 1-20 (Aamer Sohail), 2-24 (Rameez Raja), 3-163 (Javed Miandad), 4-197 (Imran Khan),5-249 (Inzamam-ul-Haq, 49.5 ov), 6-249 (Wasim Akram, 49.6 ov)

Bowling	**O**	**M**	**R**	**W**	**Econ**
DR Pringle	10	2	22	3	2.20
CC Lewis	10	2	52	0	5.20
IT Botham	7	0	42	1	6.00
PAJ DeFreitas	10	1	42	0	4.20
RK Illingworth	10	0	50	1	5.00
DA Reeve	3	0	22	0	7.33

England innings (target: 250 runs from 50 overs)		R	M	B	4s	6s	SR
GA Gooch*	c Aaqib Javed b Mushtaq Ahmed	29	93	66	1	0	43.93
IT Botham	c †Moin Khan b Wasim Akram	0	12	6	0	0	0.00
AJ Stewart†	c †Moin Khan b Aaqib Javed	7	22	16	1	0	43.75
GA Hick	lbw b Mushtaq Ahmed	17	49	36	1	0	47.22
NH Fairbrother	c †Moin Khan b Aaqib Javed	62	97	70	3	0	88.57
AJ Lamb	b Wasim Akram	31	54	41	2	0	75.60
CC Lewis	b Wasim Akram	0	6	1	0	0	0.00
DA Reeve	c Rameez Raja b Mushtaq Ahmed	15	38	32	0	0	46.87
DR Pringle	not out	18	29	16	1	0	112.50
PAJ DeFreitas	run out (Saleem Malik/ †Moin Khan)	10	13	8	0	0	125.00
RK Illingworth	c Rameez Raja b Imran Khan	14	9	10	2	0	140.00
Extras	(lb 5, w 13, nb 6)	24					
Total	(all out; 49.2 overs)	227	(4.60 runs per over)				

Fall of wickets 1-6 (Botham), 2-21 (Stewart), 3-59 (Hick), 4-69 (Gooch), 5-141 (Lamb), 6-141 (Lewis), 7-180 (Fairbrother),8-183 (Reeve), 9-208 (DeFreitas, 47.1 ov), 10-227 (Illingworth, 49.2 ov)

Bowling	**O**	**M**	**R**	**W**	**Econ**
Wasim Akram	10	0	49	3	4.90
Aaqib Javed	10	2	27	2	2.70
Mushtaq Ahmed	10	1	41	3	4.10
Ijaz Ahmed	3	0	13	0	4.33
Imran Khan	6.2	0	43	1	6.78
Aamer Sohail	10	0	49	0	4.90

1996 World Cup

Sri Lanka's Power Moment

The World Cup returned to the subcontinent after almost a decade, in a bigger and commercialised avatar. Sri Lanka was the other co-host in addition to India and Pakistan. For the first time the host country won the title.

A bomb explosion weeks before the matches and the security concerns of two of the participating countries, Australia and West Indies, shook Colombo. Both the countries refused to travel to the 'Emerald Island' and forfeited their matches. However, on the pitch, a different kind of explosion was taking place–the West Indies power was receding and the Lankan cricketers displayed the same gay abandon and aggressive strokeplay to capture the imagination of cricket fans.

Talking Points

- Australia and West Indies forfeited their matches in Colombo (SL) due to security concerns. Over a thousand people had been injured in a terrorist bomb only three weeks earlier
- In the semifinal in Kolkata at the Eden Gardens, as India slid to 120/ 8 in response to Sri Lanka's 252, the crowd started fires in the stands, leading to a win "by default" for the Lankans

The third umpire also made his first appearance in front of the TV monitor in the 1996 World Cup

Stars

Sanath Jayasuriya (SL)

The hurricane hit sixes off bowlers in the opening spell itself and swung matches in a matter of few overs, Jayasuriya deservedly won the Man of the Series, scoring 221 runs, at a strike rate of 131.54

Aravinda 'de Silva (SL)

The flamboyant vice captain was the Man of the Match in the final – 2 catches, 3 wickets and an unbeaten 107. De Silva scored an impressive 448 runs at an average of 89 in the tournament

Sachin Tendulkar (Ind)

His imperious batting before the home crowd saw his fan following reach fanatic height in spite of India's fiasco in the semis. Tendulkar emerged the highest scorer of the tournament

Remember, this was also the most widely televised World Cup so far in addition to the more expanded format of the tournament–it helped the game reach a fanatic level in the subcontinent.

The 15-over fielding restrictions had made their debut in 1992, but the pinch-hitters really came of age in the 1996 edition. Sri Lanka, India and Australia exploited the opportunity with aggressive batting in the early overs. Sri Lanka's Jayasuriya savaged Indian and English bowling attacks in the group stages. Master blaster Sachin and Australian Mark Waugh produced glorious forms.

The fan's passion spelt trouble on quite a few occasions. When Pakistan lost to India by 39 runs in the quarters held in Bangalore, back home Wasim Akram, who had dropped out of the tie due to an injury, was at the receiving end. Angry mob stoned his Lahore house. It was Aravinda de Silva's one-man show against Australia in the final which put the game back into focus. He grabbed 3 wickets and 2 catches and steered Lanka to victory with an exquisite 107 not out.

Summary

Participating Teams: Australia, England, India, New Zealand, Pakistan, South Africa, Sri Lanka, West Indies, Zimbabwe, Holland, Kenya and United Arab Emirates

Format: There were two qualifying groups of six to determine the quarterfinalists. The third umpire made his debut in front of the TV monitor.

1st SF: India v Sri Lanka at Kolkata – Mar 13, 1996 Sri Lanka 251/8 (50 ov); India 120/8 (34.1 ov); Sri Lanka won by default.

2nd SF: Australia v West Indies at Mohali - Mar 14, 1996; Australia 207/8 (50 ov); West Indies 202 (49.3 ov); Australia won by 5 runs.

"That victory brought us everything. After the victory, the other teams started giving us respect"
—Muttiah Muralitharan

Final: Australia v Sri Lanka at Lahore–Mar 17, 1996; Australia 241/7 (50 ov); Sri Lanka 245/3 (46.2 ov); Sri Lanka won by 7 wickets.

Player of the match Aravinda de Silva (Sri Lanka)
Umpires SA Bucknor and DR Shepherd

South African Gary Kirsten blasted an unbeaten 188 against UAE, which was a Cup record

Scorecard - Final

Australia innings (50 overs maximum)		R	M	B	4s	6s	SR
MA Taylor*	c Jayasuriya b de Silva	74	109	83	8	1	89.15
ME Waugh	c Jayasuriya b Vaas	12	29	15	1	0	80.00
RT Ponting	b de Silva	45	90	73	2	0	61.64
SR Waugh	c de Silva b Dharmasena	13	32	25	0	0	52.00
SK Warne	st †Kaluwitharana b Muralitharan	2	4	5	0	0	40.00
SG Law	c de Silva b Jayasuriya	22	43	30	0	1	73.33
MG Bevan	not out	36	58	49	2	0	73.46
IA Healy†	b de Silva	2	2	3	0	0	66.66
PR Reiffel	not out	13	21	18	0	0	72.22
Extras	(lb 10, w 11, nb 1)	22					
Total	(7 wickets; 50 overs)	241	(4.82 runs per over)				

Fall of wickets 1-36 (ME Waugh), 2-137 (Taylor), 3-152 (Ponting), 4-156 (Warne), 5-170 (SR Waugh), 6-202 (Law), 7-205 (Healy)

Bowling	**O**	**M**	**R**	**W**	**Econ**
GP Wickramasinghe	7	0	38	0	5.42
WPUJC Vaas	6	1	30	1	5.00
M Muralitharan	10	0	31	1	3.10
HDPK Dharmasena	10	0	47	1	4.70
ST Jayasuriya	8	0	43	1	5.37
PA de Silva	9	0	42	3	4.66

Sri Lanka innings (target: 242 runs from 50 overs)		R	M	B	4s	6s	SR
ST Jayasuriya	run out	9	9	7	1	0	128.57
RS Kaluwitharana†	c Bevan b Fleming	6	27	13	0	0	46.15
AP Gurusinha	b Reiffel	65	119	99	6	1	65.65
PA de Silva	not out	107	176	124	13	0	86.29
A Ranatunga*	not out	47	72	37	4	1	127.02
Extras	(b 1, lb 4, w 5, nb 1)	11					
Total	(3 wickets; 46.2 overs)	245	(5.28 runs per over)				

Did not bat HP Tillakaratne, RS Mahanama, HDPK Dharmasena, WPUJC Vaas, GP Wickramasinghe, M Muralitharan

Fall of wickets 1-12 (Jayasuriya), 2-23 (Kaluwitharana), 3-148 (Gurusinha)

Bowling	**O**	**M**	**R**	**W**	**Econ**
GD McGrath	8.2	1	28	0	3.36
DW Fleming	6	0	43	1	7.16
SK Warne	10	0	58	0	5.80
PR Reiffel	10	0	49	1	4.90
ME Waugh	6	0	35	0	5.83
SR Waugh	3	0	15	0	5.00
MG Bevan	3	0	12	0	4.00

1999 World Cup

Australia wins second time

The heart-stopping semifinal between Australia and South Africa is arguably one of the most memorable World Cup match. The climax, as some critic would say, came a tad bit too early, after Australia won the final against Pakistan in a one-sided fashion.

Irrespective of the team one was rooting for, the Edgbaston semifinal ranks as one of the finest in the condensed version of the game. The Proteas needed nine off the last over and Lance Klusener – on form the best batsman in that tournament – belted the first two deliveries for four. South Africa now needed one to win. The third ball went straight to a fielder, but Allan Donald was already half way down the pitch

Talking Points

- The white 'Duke' ball was introduced in the 1999 World Cup. It was claimed that the ball was harder and had more swing than the red ball
- In a Super Six match, Steve Waugh was dropped by Gibbs when the latter attempted to throw the ball in air in celebration, and the ball slipped in a hurry. Waugh went on to score an unbeaten 120 to guide Australia to a win

Bangladesh declared a national holiday back home after their team beat Pakistan in a group match

Stars

Lance Klusener (SA)

The "Zullu" was arguably the most effective player of the tournament until the fateful run out took place and left him stranded in the semifinal against Australia. He won the MVP of the tournament

Shane Warne (Aus)

The Australian leggie stole the show in the final (4/33) to emerge as the highest wicket-taker (20 wickets) along with Kiwi Geoff Allott in the tournament

Steve Waugh (Aus)

Captain courageous kept his cool when the chips were down in the early stage of the tournament and his unbeaten century helped Australia stave off an exit from the Super Six stage

and would have been run out if Darren Lehmann had hit the stumps.

The fourth wasn't much of a shot either, but Klusener said "yes". Donald disagreed and didn't budge. As Klusener passed him, Donald realised he had to go, but it was too late. Donald was run out, South Africa were all out, the scores were tied and Australia progressed to the final thanks to an earlier win over South Africa.

It was the most lop-sided final! Pakistan collapsed for a paltry 132, the lowest total ever recorded in a World Cup final with Glenn McGrath and man of the match Shane Warne creating maximum damage. In response, the Australians lost just two wickets as they knocked off the runs in a businesslike fashion.

Some of the other highlights were Bangladesh shocking the runners-up in a group match. The West Indies'downfall was evident strongly and they made an early exit again. Sachin Tendulkar's noble gesture to return to action after the loss of his father in between the tournament was an unforgettable act.

Summary

Participating Teams: Australia, England, India, New Zealand, Pakistan, South Africa, Sri Lanka, West Indies, Zimbabwe, Bangladesh, Kenya, Scotland

Format: The 12 contestants were divided into two groups, in each of which teams played each other in the league stage. The top-3 from each group advanced to the Super Sixes, a new concept brought about in this World Cup, where each qualifier from group A played with each qualifier from group B. The teams also carried forward their points from games against each qualifer from their group. The top-4 in the Super Sixes contested the semifinals.

"The (semifinal tie against South Africa) best game of cricket I have played"

– Steve Waugh

1st SF: New Zealand v Pakistan at Manchester - June 16, 1999; Pakistan won by 9 wickets. New Zealand 241-7 (50 ov); Pakistan 242-1 (47.3 ov).

2nd SF: Australia v South Africa at Birmingham - June 17, 1999; Match tied. Australia 213 (49.2 ov); South Africa 213 (49.4 ov).

Final: Australia beat Pakistan by 8 wickets

Rahul Dravid was the highest scorer with 461 runs while Geoff Allot and Warne were the highest wicket-taker with 20 each

Scorecard - Final

Pakistan innings (50 overs maximum)		R	M	B	4s	6s	SR
Saeed Anwar	b Fleming	15	26	17	3	0	88.23
Wajahatullah Wasti	c ME Waugh b McGrath	1	20	14	0	0	7.14
Abdul Razzaq	c SR Waugh b Moody	17	67	51	2	0	33.33
Ijaz Ahmed	b Warne	22	79	46	2	0	47.82
Inzamam-ul-Haq	c †Gilchrist b Reiffel	15	47	33	0	0	45.45
Moin Khan†	c †Gilchrist b Warne	6	16	12	0	0	50.00
Shahid Afridi	lbw b Warne	13	22	16	2	0	81.25
Azhar Mahmood	c & b Moody	8	32	17	1	0	47.05
Wasim Akram*	c SR Waugh b Warne	8	23	20	0	1	40.00
Saqlain Mushtaq	c Ponting b McGrath	0	10	4	0	0	0.00
Shoaib Akhtar	not out	2	8	6	0	0	33.33
Extras	(lb 10, w 13, nb 2)	25					
Total	(all out; 39 overs)	132	(3.38 runs per over)				

Fall of wickets 1-21 (Wajahatullah Wasti, 4.4 ov), 2-21 (Saeed Anwar, 5.1 ov), 3-68 (Abdul Razzaq, 19.4 ov), 4-77 (Ijaz Ahmed, 23.4 ov), 5-91 (Moin Khan, 27.1 ov), 6-104 (Inzamam-ul-Haq, 30.1 ov), 7-113 (Shahid Afridi, 31.6 ov), 8-129 (Azhar Mahmood, 36.6 ov), 9-129 (Wasim Akram, 37.2 ov), 10-132 (Saqlain Mushtaq, 38.6 ov)

Bowling	O	M	R	W	Econ
GD McGrath	9	3	13	2	1.44
DW Fleming	6	0	30	1	5.00
PR Reiffel	10	1	29	1	2.90
TM Moody	5	0	17	2	3.40
SK Warne	9	1	33	4	3.66

Australia innings (target: 133 runs from 50 overs)		R	M	B	4s	6s	SR
ME Waugh	not out	37	95	52	4	0	71.15
AC Gilchrist†	c Inzamam-ul-Haq b Saqlain Mushtaq	54	49	36	8	1	150.00
RT Ponting	c †Moin Khan b Wasim Akram	24	32	27	3	0	88.88
DS Lehmann	not out	13	12	9	2	0	144.44
Extras	(lb 1, w 1, nb 3)	5					
Total	(2 wickets; 20.1 overs)	133	(6.59 runs per over)				

Did not bat SR Waugh*, MG Bevan, TM Moody, SK Warne, PR Reiffel, DW Fleming, GD McGrath

Fall of wickets 1-75 (Gilchrist, 10.1 ov), 2-112 (Ponting, 17.4 ov)

Bowling	**O**	**M**	**R**	**W**	**Econ**
Wasim Akram	8	1	41	1	5.12
Shoaib Akhtar	4	0	37	0	9.25
Abdul Razzaq	2	0	13	0	6.50
Azhar Mahmood	2	0	20	0	10.00
Saqlain Mushtaq	4.1	0	21	1	5.04

2003 World Cup

India's heartbreak

Erratic fielding and bowling in the final dashed India's dream of repeating the 1983 feat. Unlike then, there were more experienced one-day specialists in the squad this time, the Kolkata Test win against Australia was still afresh in the memory and thousands of fans descended in South Africa sniffing victory in the air. While Kapil's Devils had everyone contributing, the dependency on just one star player to keep winning matches backfired.

Talking Points

- Australia's Shane Warne failed a drug test and had to fly home a day before their opening match. Warne had tested positive for a banned diuretic
- Zimbabwea's Andy Flower and Henry Olonga (the former white, the latter black) wore black armbands for their opening tie, explaining that they were "mourning the death of democracy in Zimbabwe"

The imperious batting of Sachin Tendulkar deservedly earned him the man of the series award, but the others were required to fire more frequently. On the other hand, Australia minus Steve Waugh and Shane Warne, played like champions, routing India by

Sachin Tendulkar was the highest scorer in the Cup (673 runs) and also won the man of the series award

Stars

Ricky Ponting (Aus)

Australian skipper Ricky Ponting led from the front, playing the knock of his life for an unbeaten 140 that powered Australia to 359 for just 2 wickets from 50 overs.

Glenn McGrath (Aus)

The terminator, McGrath chimed in with 3 wickets as the Australian skittled India for 234 in 39.2 overs. McGrath took 3 important wickets in the final against India.

Sachin Tendulkar (Ind)

The master blaster was the highest scorer in the 2003 Wrodl Cup with 673 runs and desrevingly won the man of the series award..

125 runs to win the World Cup for a historic third time.

Australian skipper Ricky Ponting led from the front, playing the knock of his life for an unbeaten 140 that powered Australia to 359 for just two wickets from 50 overs in the final. Adam Gilchrist and Hayden took 15 runs off the first over bowled by Zaheer Khan, and the bowler looked lost for the rest of the day at the Wanderers. Javagal Srinath was smashed for five fours and a six before he was taken off the attack and the third pacer Ashish Nehra didn't go cheaply either.

The thousands of Indian fans present at the stadium were pining their hopes on the indepth batting order, but the score was simply beyond their reach. Tendulkar was dismissed cheaply in the first over to McGrath, who recalls their duel till date as one of his finest. Rearguard action from Virender Sehwag, Sourav Ganguly and Rahul Dravid in two different partnerships, divine interruption from the rain provided illusions to a foregone conclusion.

Summary

Participating Teams: India, England, Pakistan, Australia, Zimbabwe, Netherlands, Namibia, New Zealand, West Indies, Sri Lanka, Kenya, South Africa, Canada, Bangladesh.

Format: The contestants were divided into two pools- and the Top-3 teams from each group advanced to the Super Six, carrying the results against other qualifiers to that round. The Top-4 teams of Super Six played the semifinals and the winners clashed in the finals.

1st SF: Australia v Sri Lanka at Port Elizabeth - Mar 18, 2003; Australia 212/7 (50 ov); Sri Lanka 123/7 (38.1/38.1 ov); Australia won by 48 runs (D/L method).

> "It's a regret... It still hurts, but there is also a positive side - that I led Team India to the final"
>
> —Sourav Ganguly

2nd SF: India v Kenya at Durban - Mar 20, 2003 India 270/4 (50 ov) beat Kenya 179 (46.2 ov) by 91 runs.

Final: Australia 359/2 (50 ov) beat India 234 (39.2 ov) by 125 runs.
Player of the match RT Ponting (Australia).
Umpires SA Bucknor (West Indies) and DR Shepherd (England).

India conceded as many as 37 extras in the final against Australia

Scorecard - Final

Australia innings (50 overs maximum)		R	M	B	4s	6s	SR
AC Gilchrist†	c Sehwag b Harbhajan	57	66	48	8	1	118.75
ML Hayden	c †Dravid b Harbhajan	37	93	54	5	0	68.51
RT Ponting*	not out	140	138	121	4	8	115.70
DR Martyn	not out	88	112	84	7	1	104.76
Extras	(b 2, lb 12, w 16, nb 7)	37					
Total	(2 wickets; 50 overs; 205 mins)	359	(7.18 runs per over)				

Did not bat DS Lehmann, MG Bevan, A Symonds, GB Hogg, AJ Bichel, B Lee, GD McGrath

Fall of wickets 1-105 (Gilchrist, 13.6 ov), 2-125 (Hayden, 19.5 ov)

Bowling	**O**	**M**	**R**	**W**	**Econ**
Z Khan	7	0	67	0	9.57
J Srinath	10	0	87	0	8.70
A Nehra	10	0	57	0	5.70
Harbhajan Singh	8	0	49	2	6.12
V Sehwag	3	0	14	0	4.66
SR Tendulkar	3	0	20	0	6.66
D Mongia	7	0	39	0	5.57
Yuvraj Singh	2	0	12	0	6.00

India innings (target: 360 runs from 50 overs)		R	M	B	4s	6s	SR
SR Tendulkar	c & b McGrath	4	2	5	1	0	80.00
V Sehwag	run out (Lehmann)	82	107	81	10	3	101.23
SC Ganguly*	c Lehmann b Lee	24	44	25	3	1	96.00
M Kaif	c †Gilchrist b McGrath	0	4	3	0	0	0.00
R Dravid†	b Bichel	47	87	57	2	0	82.45
Yuvraj Singh	c Lee b Hogg	24	48	34	1	0	70.58
D Mongia	c Martyn b Symonds	12	18	11	2	0	109.09
Harbhajan Singh	c McGrath b Symonds	7	12	8	0	0	87.50
Z Khan	c Lehmann b McGrath	4	20	8	0	0	50.00
J Srinath	b Lee	1	6	4	0	0	25.00
A Nehra	not out	8	7	4	2	0	200.00
Extras	(b 4, lb 4, w 9, nb 4)	21					
Total	(all out; 39.2 overs; 180 mins)		234	(5.94 runs per over)			

Did not bat HP Tillakaratne, RS Mahanama, HDPK Dharmasena, WPUJC Vaas, GP Wickramasinghe, M Muralitharan

Fall of wickets 1-4 (Tendulkar, 0.5 ov), 2-58 (Ganguly, 9.5 ov), 3-59 (Kaif, 10.3 ov), 4-147 (Sehwag, 23.5 ov),5-187 (Dravid, 31.5 ov), 6-208 (Yuvraj Singh, 34.5 ov), 7-209 (Mongia, 35.2 ov), 8-223 (Harbhajan Singh, 37.1 ov),9-226 (Srinath, 38.2 ov), 10-234 (Khan, 39.2 ov)

Bowling	**O**	**M**	**R**	**W**	**Econ**
GD McGrath	8.2	0	52	3	6.24
B Lee	7	1	31	2	4.42
GB Hogg	10	0	61	1	6.10
DS Lehmann	2	0	18	0	9.00
AJ Bichel	10	0	57	1	5.70
A Symonds	2	0	7	2	3.50

2007 World Cup

Historic fourth for Australia

Shocking upsets, a gory murder mystery and controversial umpiring in the rain-interrupted final which was played in almost darkness, the World Cup in 2007 seemed hazy and mismanaged. While it was a forgettable tournament for many reasons, the unforgettable part was the indomitable Australians' third title in a row, fourth overall. Australia also carried their winning streak to 29 consecutive World Cup matches without loss, a streak dating back to the group stage of the 1999 edition.

Talking Points

- A murder mystery rocked the cricket world after Pakistan coach Bob Woolmer was found dead in his hotel room the day after his team's shock defeat against Ireland
- England's Andrew Flintoff was fired from vice captaincy and dropped from the match against Canada and several of his teammates fined for breaking a team curfew

The final was a repeat of the 1996 World Cup – Australia vs Sri Lanka. The Lankans thrashed the Kiwis by 81 runs in the first semifinal and the Australia versus South Africa semifinal proved to be a no-contest.

South Africa's Herschelle Gibbs hit six sixes in one Daan van Bunge over against the Netherlands

Stars

Glenn McGrath (Aus)

The chief architect of Australia's record title, McGrath was the leading wicket-taker in the tournament (26) and also overtook Wasim Akram's record haul of 55 wickets overall in the World Cup

Matthew Hayden (Aus)

The tall Australian opener was the standout batsman of the tournament as he smashed 659 runs with three centuries, including a 66- ball ton against South Africa - the fastest in World Cup history

Adam Gilchrist (Aus)

The attacking Gilchrist finished his innings in the final with a majestic knock of 149 runs. He smashed 13 fours and eight sixes en route his innings and Australia were sitting on top.

The final was a 38-over affair due to early rain and eventually decided by the Duckworth-Lewis (D-L) method after more rain disrupted play. Australia's Adam Gilchrist launched a blitzkrieg which shell-shocked the Lankan bowlers. When Gilchrist finished his innings at 149 runs, he had smashed 13 fours and eight sixes, and Australia were sitting on top at 281 for four. Lankans Kumara Sangakkara and Sanath Jayasuriya added 116 for the second wicket but their hopes were slowly washed away, and more rains turned the final farcical. The officials insisted that 36 overs had to be bowled to complete the match and in the end, Australia won by 53-run via the D-L method.

The tournament was stifled for many reasons – overpriced tickets, long duration, and also the fact that two of the biggest draws, India and Pakistan made a hurried exit. The upset at the hands of Bangladesh in the opening game put India under tremendous pressure and though they piled on batting records against Bermuda, they had to pack up their bags after losing to Sri Lanka in the next game.

Summary

Participating Teams: Australia, Bangladesh, Bermuda, Canada, England, Holland (Netherlands), India, Ireland, Kenya, New Zealand, Pakistan, Scotland, South Africa, Sri Lanka, West Indies, Zimbabwe

Format: The top two teams in each group proceeded to the Super 8 stage which was played on a league system, with the top four teams qualifying for the semifinals.

1st SF: New Zealand v Sri Lanka at Kingston - Apr 24, 2007; Sri Lanka 289/5 (50 ov) beat New Zealand 208 (41.4 ov) by 81 runs.

2nd SF: Australia v South Africa at Gros Islet - Apr 25, 2007; South Africa 149 (43.5 ov) beat Australia 153/3 (31.3 ov) by 7 wickets.

Final: Australia v Sri Lanka at Bridgetown - Apr 28, 2007; Australia 281/4 (38/38 ov) beat Sri Lanka 215/8 (36/36 ov); by 53 runs.

"They (Australia) have been indestructible and etched themselves in history as arguably the greatest one-day team ever"

– Steve Waugh, Australian captain

India scored 413/5 against Bermuda, breaking the World Cup record for the highest team total

Scorecard - Final

Australia innings (38 overs maximum)		R	M	B	4s	6s	SR
AC Gilchrist†	c Silva b Fernando	149	129	104	13	8	143.26
ML Hayden	c Jayawardene b Malinga	38	100	55	3	1	69.09
RT Ponting*	run out (Jayawardene)	37	53	42	1	1	88.09
A Symonds	not out	23	39	21	2	0	109.52
SR Watson	b Malinga	3	3	3	0	0	100.00
MJ Clarke	not out	8	10	6	1	0	133.33
Extras	(lb 4, w 16, nb 3)	23					
Total	(4 wickets; 38 overs; 169 mins)	281	(7.39 runs per over)				

Did not bat MEK Hussey, GB Hogg, NW Bracken, SW Tait, GD McGrath

Fall of wickets 1-172 (Hayden, 22.5 ov), 2-224 (Gilchrist, 30.3 ov), 3-261 (Ponting, 35.4 ov), 4-266 (Watson, 36.2 ov)

Bowling	**O**	**M**	**R**	**W**	**Econ**
WPUJC Vaas	8	0	54	0	6.75
SL Malinga	8	1	49	2	6.12
CRD Fernando	8	0	74	1	9.25
M Muralitharan	7	0	44	0	6.28
TM Dilshan	2	0	23	0	11.50
ST Jayasuriya	5	0	33	0	6.60

Sri Lanka innings (target: 269 runs from 36 overs)		R	M	B	4s	6s	SR
WU Tharanga	c †Gilchrist b Bracken	6	11	8	1	0	75.00
ST Jayasuriya	b Clarke	63	108	67	9	0	94.02
KC Sangakkara†	c Ponting b Hogg	54	72	52	6	1	103.84
DPMD Jayawardene*	lbw b Watson	19	31	19	1	0	100.00
LPC Silva	b Clarke	21	41	22	1	1	95.45
TM Dilshan	run out (Clarke/McGrath)	14	20	13	2	0	107.69
RP Arnold	c †Gilchrist b McGrath	1	9	2	0	0	50.00
WPUJC Vaas	not out	11	20	21	0	0	52.38
SL Malinga	st †Gilchrist b Symonds	10	6	6	0	1	166.66
CRD Fernando	not out	1	6	6	0	0	16.66
Extras	(lb 1, w 14)	15					
Total	(8 wickets; 36 overs; 171 mins)		215	(5.97 runs per over)			

Did not bat M Muralitharan

Fall of wickets 1-7 (Tharanga, 2.1 ov), 2-123 (Sangakkara, 19.5 ov), 3-145 (Jayasuriya, 22.6 ov),4-156 (Jayawardene, 25.5 ov), 5-188 (Dilshan, 29.6 ov), 6-190 (Silva, 30.1 ov), 7-194 (Arnold, 31.5 ov),8-211 (Malinga, 33.6 ov)

Bowling	O	M	R	W	Econ
NW Bracken	6	1	34	1	5.66
SW Tait	6	0	42	0	7.00
GD McGrath	7	0	31	1	4.42
SR Watson	7	0	49	1	7.00
GB Hogg	3	0	19	1	6.33
MJ Clarke	5	0	33	2	6.60
A Symonds	2	0	6	1	3.00

2011 World Cup The 14 Teams

1

Australia

CRICKET
AUSTRALIA

Team Squad

Ricky Ponting (captain), Michael Clarke (vice-captain), Doug Bollinger, Brad Haddin (wicket-keeper), John Hastings, Nathan Hauritz, David Hussey, Mike Hussey, Mitchell Johnson, Brett Lee, Tim Paine (wicket-keeper), Steve Smith, Shaun Tait, Shane Watson, Cameron White.

Ricky Ponting (Captain)

The 'Punter' remains the most successful captain of his country despite constant criticism about his captaincy. His three World Cup titles and two Champions Trophy victory should squash any debate on the quality of his leadership, though there is no doubt that the Australians aren't looking as invincible as the previous edition. Ponting is also racing to be fit for the Cup after fracturing his little finger in the Ashes series. He is the third-most prolific run scorer in ODIs, and his aggressive batting could play an important factor in Australia's attempt to win their fifth World Cup.

Tim Nielsen (Coach)

He will find it tough to emulate the achievement of his predecessor, John Buchanan, but the 43-year-old former South Australia state cricketer is realistic about his chances. Nielsen took over the mantle post-2007 World Cup and believes that Shane Warne and Glen McGrath cannot be replaced but that "we need to make sure we have 12 to 15 players coming and trying to move forward together as a group and try to replace the 1200 wickets in maybe little bits and pieces."

2
Bangladesh

বাংলাদেশ

Bangladesh Cricket Board

Team Squad

Shakib Al Hasan (captain), Tamim Iqbal (vice-captain), Shahriar Nafees, Imrul Kayes, Mohammad Ashraful, Zunaed Siddique, Roqibul Hassan, Mushfiqur Rahim, Naeem Islam, Mahmudullah, Abdur Razzak, Rubel Hossain, Shafiul Islam, Nazmul Hossain, Md Sohrawordi.

Shakib Al Hasan (Captain)

Bangladesh football's loss has been cricket's gain, and that for a player who went on to become Wisden's Test Player of the Year in 2009. The Bangladeshi captain showed early promise in the most popular sport of the world but cricket's future was brighter in this part. The 24-year all-rounder who is a left-handed batsman and orthodox spinner also has the distinction of securing his team's first overseas series win against the West Indies. Hasan has the unenviable task of rallying his players after the surprise omission of former captain and fast bowler Mashrafe Mortaza for the tournament.

Jamie Siddons (Coach)

A versatile sportsman who played Australian Rules Football, Siddons scored more than 11,000 runs for Victoria and South Australia during his playing career but his only international recognition came in a one-day game against Pakistan in 1988. Siddons took over from Dave Whatmore in 2007, and has boosted the young team's confidence since then. Bangladesh's run-up to the World Cup has been good so far and they are currently ranked No.8 in the ODI ranking. Siddons has the task of inspiring a team that surprisingly beat India and South Africa in the 2007 World Cup.

3

Canada

CRICKET
CANADA

Team Squad

Ashish Bagai (captain), Rizwan Cheema (vice-captain), Harvir Baidwan, Khurram Chohan, Ruvindu Gunaskera, John Davison, Hiral Patel, Nitish Kumar, Parth Desai, Tyson Gordon, Amarbir Hansra, Henry Osinde, Balaji Rao, Zubin Surkari, Karl.

Ashish Bagai (Captain)

The 29-year-old Canadian, who put his career as an investment banker on hold to focus on cricket, has plenty of personal experience on the international scene. The Delhi-born made his debut for Canada at the age of 17 and has since played in the 2003 and 2007 World Cups, playing a total of 54 ODI caps, 1,736 runs in ODIs, including two centuries and 14 fifties. Playing their fourth World Cup, Canada have failed to make a serious impact despite a famous win over Bangladesh in 2003. Bagai aims for a slot in the second round – the rich experience could count for his young team.

Pubudu Dassanayake (Coach)

For the former Sri Lankan player and now Canada's coach, priming the players to perform on the big stage has been the key to preparation. The 41-year-old Dassanayake played 11 Tests and 16 ODIs from 1993-94. He also played for Canada in the ICC Trophy averaging 15.20 with the bat and accounted for eight dismissals (5 catches/3 stumpings). In August 2007, Dassanayake took over as the full-time coach of Canada, replacing Andy Pick. The Lankan is confident that his players will feel at home on the subcontinent pitches – 10 of his players have their roots in Asia.

4
England

ENGLAND
CRICKET

Team Squad

Andrew Strauss (captain), Matt Prior (wicketkeeper), Ian Bell, Paul Collingwood, Tim Bresnan, Eoin Morgan, Kevin Pietersen, James Tredwell, Luke Wright, Graeme Swann, Jonathan Trott, Michael Yardy, James Anderson, Stuart Broad, Ajmal Shahzad.

Andrew Strauss (Captain)

England will be hoping to break the jinx – they have reached the final thrice, and Strauss will be hoping to be the first English captain to hold the trophy. The left-handed opening batsman quickly rose to fame on his Test debut against New Zealand in 2004, his ODI debut happened a year earlier. On Test debut, he became only the fourth England batsman to score a century and played a major role in that victory over New Zealand. Strauss is less sceptic than the critics about England's record on the subcontinent pitches and feels "England can surprise their opponents".

Andy Flower (Coach)

One of the finest cricketers to emerge from Zimbabwe, Andy Flower (one half of the Flower brothers) joined the English think-tank as assistant coach in 2007 and moved upward as team director in 2009. England went on to win the 2009 Ashes and the 2010 ICC World T20 tournament. Flower has some great memories of playing in the subcontinent, and he needs to transfer that confidence to his players for the 2011 Cup. He holds the Zimbabwean records for the most Test career runs, the highest Test batting average, and most ODI career runs, as a coach it would be perfect icing on the cake if England can win the title.

5
India

Team Squad

MS Dhoni (captain & wicket-keeper), Sachin Tendulkar, Virender Sehwag, Gautam Gambhir, Yuvraj Singh, Suresh Raina, Virat Kohli, Yusuf Pathan, Zaheer Khan, Ashish Nehra, Munaf Patel, S Sreesanth, Harbhajan Singh, R. Ashwin, Piyush Chawla.

MS Dhoni (Captain)

Mahendra Singh Dhoni's meteoric rise has become part of cricket's folklore in small-town India but the redoubtable 'MSD' now faces the Himalayan task of keeping his billion countrymen happy.

From the time he marauded the Pakistani 'A' attack in Nairobi and walked into the consciousness of a nation devoted for life to Sachin Tendulkar, Dhoni has survived the Doubting Thomases many times – the World Cup T20 title, his long run with the Indian captaincy, rising stocks in the IPL with the Chennai Super Kings, more advertising contracts and an increasing number of bikes in the backyard, 'Mahi' would be hoping to emulate the achievement of another small-town hero by the name of Kapil Dev.

Gary Kirsten (Coach)

Someone needs to thank the guy who first gave the nod to Kirsten's CV for the Indian coach's job. His self-effacing nature, but direct to the point fits in perfectly with the star-studded Indian team, surrounded for ever by hype and pressure. As a player for South Africa, Kirsten played his role according to his strength and weakness, without giving anyone much chance to complain about the lack of flair in his batting. He went on to play 101 Tests and 185 ODIs for the Proteas. Strong chances that as a coach he will also achieve his goal with India.

6
Ireland

CRICKET
IRELAND

Team Squad

William Porterfield (captain), Andre Botha, Alex Cusack, Niall O'Brien (wk), Kevin O'Brien, George Dockrell, Trent Johnston, Nigel Jones, John Mooney, Boyd Rankin, Paul Stirling, Albert van der Merwe, Gary Wilson (wicketkeeper), Andrew White, Ed Joyce.

William Porterfield (Captain)

Ireland will look up to their 27-year-old skipper to remind everyone that their win against Bangladesh in 2007 World Cup was not a mere fluke. Porterfield hit two centuries in succession early in his one-day career, 112 not out to guide his team to victory over Bermuda and an unbeaten 104 against Kenya. In a 2007 World Cup Super 8 game, Ireland shocked Bangladesh with Porterfield contributing a handsome 85 which fetched him the man of the match award. The left-hander was appointed Ireland captain at the start of the 2008 season, succeeding Trent Johnston.

Phil Simmons (Coach)

"Big Phil", who took over as head coach of Ireland after the 2007 World Cup, believes his team is better placed than even the previous edition. Simmons was a skilful opener and a useful bowler for the West Indies side in the eighties. His career didn't take off on an auspicious note but he went on to represent the Windies in 26 Test matches and 143 ODIs before a hit on the head on the England tour stopped his playing career in 1988. After recovery he took up coaching and moved to Ireland after a controversial stint with Zimbabwe.

7

Kenya

CRICKET KENYA

Team Squad

Jimmy Kamande (captain), Seren Waters, Alex Obanda, Elijah Otieno, Rakep Patel, David Obuya, Collins Obuya, Steve Tikolo, Tamnay Mishra, Maurice Ouma, Nehemiah Odhiambo, Thomas Odoyo, Shem Ngoche, James Ngoche, Peter Ongondo.

Jimmy Kamande (Captain)

The Kenyan skipper's determination to play for his country stands out. Kamanade's career took off when he was selected to play in the 1999 World Cup at the age of 21, but his career ran into problem when his bowling action came under scanner in 2004. Most cricketers playing for an Associate nation would have switched jobs, Kamanade transformed himself from a medium-fast bowler to an off-spinner, controlled his action and walked into the Kenyan team again. The Kenyan skipper is also a useful batsman with a highest score of 74 in ODIs.

Eldine Baptiste(Coach)

The owner of probably one of the most enviable record, Baptiste, largely unknown to the cricket fans except now as Kenya coach, had featured in 10 Test matches for the West Indies in the eighties – and they won all of them. He switched over to coaching and years later, took charge of a Kenyan team in transition in 2009. Kenya are struggling to erase the memories of poor performance at the 2007 WC and ICC World Twenty20, and it remains to be seen whether Baptiste can bring luck for them.

8

The Netherlands

Team Squad

Peter Borren (captain.), Wesley Barresi (wicketkeeper), Adeel Raja, Atse Buurman (wicketkeeper), Mudassar Bukhari, Ryan ten Doeschate, Tom Cooper, Alexei Kervezee, Bradley Kruger, Bernard Loots, Pieter Seelaar, Tom de Grooth, Eric Szwarczynski, Berend Westdijk, Bas Zuiderent.

Peter William Borren (Captain)

Another captain who was born in a country known for its cricket lineage but opted to play for an Associate nation. Borren was born in Christchurch and even played for New Zealand in the Under-19 World Cup in 2001-02 before moving to the Netherland. A right-handed batsman and a useful bowler, "Baldrick" as he is called by teammates, was the catalyst of the last-ball win against England in the 2007 ICC World Twenty20. He grabbed the crucial wicket of Eoin Morgan and then smashed 30 in 25 balls, including a mighty six off Paul Collingwood.

Peter Drinnen (Coach)

The former Queensland cricketer switched to coaching early in his career and was the national coach of Scotland which he had to quit in controversial circumstances. The former right-handed batsman-cum-wicketkeeper then joined Netherland in 2008, replacing Peter Cantrell, who stepped down after the 2007 World Cup.

9
New Zealand

NEW ZEALAND
CRICKET

Team Squad

Daniel Vettori (captain), Hamish Bennett, James Franklin, Martin Guptill, Jamie How, Brendon McCullum, Nathan McCullum, Kyle Mills, Jacob Oram, Jesse Ryder, Tim Southee, Scott Styris, Ross Taylor, Kane Williamson, Luke Woodcock.

Daniel Luca Vettori (Captain)

The youngest cricketer to play for New Zealand at 18, Vettori is among the handful of players who has achieved the rare 'double' of 3000 runs and 300 wickets in Test matches and 2000 runs and 200 wickets in ODIs. Master of the drift and flight and controlled length, the 31-year-old left-arm spinner is the most dangerous Kiwi bowler in the side. Vettori succeeded Stephen Fleming in 2007 and is hoping to take New Zealand to their first-ever final with the support of John Wright, who coached India to the 2003 WC final.

John Wright (Coach)

The man who coached India from 2000 to 2005 sits on the saddle for New Zealand, armed with a lot of information on the subcontinent conditions, pitches and a few dressing room tricks. Wright is fondly remembered in India as the coach who gave valuable direction to the protean talent of the Indian team. New Zealand's previous visit to the subcontinent was forgettable as they were thrashed by both India and Bangladesh. Irrespective of whether the Kiwis win or not, Wright will remain a crowd favourite.

10
Pakistan

Team Squad

Shahid Afridi (captain), Misbah-ul-Haq (vice-captain), Muhammad Hafeez, Kamran Akmal, Younis Khan, Asad Shafiq, Umer Akmal, Abdul Razzaq, Abdul Rehman, Saeed Ajmal, Shoaib Akhtar, Umer Gul, Wahab Riaz, Junaid Khan, Ahmed Shehzad.

Shahid Afridi (Captain)

The explosive Pathan takes batting into another realm. Afridi has two of the fastest century in ODIs to his credit, including the fastest. A cricketer made for the condensed version, Afridi has smashed 288 sixes in his ODI career and was the player of the tournament in the inaugural ICC World Twenty20 and returned two years later to win the championship. If that's not enough then he owns the traditional leg-break and two googlies with lethal impact. His real challenge, though, would be to keep the tempestuous Pakistani side in the World Cup on track.

Waqar Younis (Coach)

The former bowling great, who bagged almost 800 wickets combining both ODIs and Test matches, comes into the job at a difficult time. Younis, known for his expressway speed and focus on hitting the stumps rather than the batsman had another unusual trait–putting the reverse in the swing. His biggest challenge at the 2011 World Cup would be to swing it for Pakistani cricket in its most adverse conditions.

11
South Africa

Team Squad

Graeme Smith (captain), Hashim Amla, Johan Botha, AB de Villiers (wicket-keeper), JP Duminy, Faf du Plessis, Colin Ingram, Jacques Kallis, Morne Morkel, Wayne Parnell, Robbie Peterson, Dale Steyn, Imran Tahir, Lonwabo Tsotsobe, Morne van Wyk (wicket-keeper).

Graeme Smith (Captain)

Smith has seen it all from an early age. He was given the task of rebuilding South African cricket at just 22 years of age after the 2003 World Cup faced relentless criticism for his side's debacles but his growth in the role was noticed when he was asked to lead the ICC World XI versus Australia in a couple of years time. That year he led the Proteas through 20 consecutive undefeated ODI games. The left-hander with more than 6,000 runs in ODIs has played many fine knocks in all forms of the game, and now he needs to produce a special one to lead his side to their first Cup title.

Corrie van Zyl (Coach)

The former right-arm fast bowler outlines consistency as the primary aim for his team in the 2011 World Cup. Zyl, who made a delayed debut in the international area due to the apartheid ban, played three Tests and two ODIS. He took over the coach's job just days ahead of their India tour in 2010. That opportunity has given him a clearer picture of what his team needs to do to be a force in the subcontinent at the World Cup.

12
Sri Lanka

Team Squad

Kumar Sangakkara (captain), Mahela Jayawardene (vice-captain), Tillakaratne Dilshan, Upul Tharanga, Thilan Samaraweera, Chamara Silva, Chamara Kapugedera, Angelo Mathews, Thisara Perera, Nuwan Kulasekara, Lasith Malinga, Dilhara Fernando, Muttiah Muralitharan, Ajantha Mendis, Rangana Herath.

Kumar Choksanada Sangakkara (Captain)

It wouldn't be incorrect to say that the Lankan skipper faces an equally daunting task as MS Dhoni and Shahid Afridi . The pressure of playing in the subcontinent is such that Sangakkara has two choices–of emulating Arjuna Ranatunga's feat in the 1996 World Cup or improving his predecessor Sanath Jayasuriya's record in the 2007 edition where Lanka finished runners-up. The 33-year-old left-hander has a fantastic record in all forms of the game, is a multi-tasker and a cool customer when it comes to handling sledging tactics. The suave Sangakkara will feel the heat as Sri Lanka makes a bid to win their second World Cup.

Trevor Bayliss (Coach)

The former New South Wales (Australia) middle-order batsman and a brilliant cover fielder succeeded Tom Moody as the coach of the Sri Lankan team in 2007. Since then Bayliss has played a major role in improving Sri Lanka's ranking in both Test and ODIs, his primary mantra being consistency. Sri Lanka's foreign expert admits that the World Cup is a very big thing in the island and "everyone involved in cricket would like to copy what happened in 1996".

13
West Indies

Team Squad

Darren Sammy (captain), Adrian Barath, Carlton Baugh Jr, Sulieman Benn, Darren Bravo, Dwayne Bravo, Shivnarine Chanderpaul, Chris Gayle, Nikita Miller, Kieron Pollard, Ravi Rampaul, Kemar Roach, Andre Russell, Ramnaresh Sarwan, Devon Smith.

Darren Julius Garvey Sammy (Captain)

It's quite unusual in recent times for an all-rounder to be appointed the captain of the West Indies. But then it is also unusual for St. Lucia, one of the Caribbean islands, to produce an international cricketer. Sammy was appointed as captain of the West Indies in October 2010 after Chris Gayle and Dwayne Bravo refused to sign a central contract with the West Indies Cricket Board. Sammy, who is a right-handed batsman and a fast-medium bowler made his international debut against New Zealand in 2004 in an odd fashion–the ODI was washed away without a single ball being bowled.

Ottis Gibson (Coach)

The former West Indies international known for his intelligent bowling with the old ball and lusty hitting took to coaching early in his career. Gibson also happens to be one of the 79 players who have scalped all 10 wickets in an innings for Durham, playing against Hampshire. It is been 15 years since West Indies cricket has been in the doldrums and Gibson feels, "it will take at least five years to get back to where we want to". The process has to begin somewhere and the World Cup could be the best place to take off.

14
Zimbabwe

zimbabwe cricket

Team Squad

Elton Chigumbura (captain.), Brendan Taylor, Regis Chakabva, Charles Coventry, Graeme Cremer, Craig Ervine, Sean Ervine, Gregory Lamb, Shingirai Masakadza, Tatenda Taibu (wicketkeeper), Edward Rainsford, Prosper Utseya, Raymond Price, Christopher Mpofu and Sean Williams.

Elton Chigumbura (Captain)

Zimbabwe's leading all-rounder has the knack of being at the right place at the right time. He made his mark as a member of the Zimbabwean team, which shocked Australia in the Under-19 World Cup held in Bangladesh. His international debut came earlier than expected, at the age of 18, due to the absence of the 'rebel' players. Chigumbura was part of the Zimbabwean squad for the 2007 World Cup. He registered new career-best ODI bowling figures of 3 for 25 and scored 38 runs from 34 balls in Zimbabwe's shock win against the West Indies. Now it remains to be seen whether he is the right man to lead Zimbabwe out of the transition process.

Alan Butcher (Coach)

The person in charge of mentoring Zimbabwe honed his formative skills in Australia and played most of his cricket for Surrey (England) and later Glamorgan. Butcher was selected for England in only one Test, against India at the Oval in 1979, and he switched to coaching after retiring from country cricket. Zimbabwe has progressed beyond the group stage only twice in the World Cup but Butcher is hopeful that "the turnaround is in the process".

Strengths, Weaknesses & Teams' Records

AUSTRALIA

Ricky Ponting (Captain)

Best World Cup performance

Champions in 1987, 1999, 2003, 2007

Captain

Ricky Ponting

Coach

Tim Nielsen

World Cup win-loss record

51-17, 1 tie

Key Players

Ricky Ponting, Brett Lee, Cameron White

Strengths

The Australians are No. 1 in the ODI rankings, went through the 2007 World Cup undefeated, and has the best win-loss ratio in the quadrennial tournament. Ricky Ponting, who has played in the last four World Cup finals and stands second behind Sachin Tendulkar in the run list, is back at the helm after nursing a broken finger which sidelined him since late December. Australia thrashed archrivals England 6-1 in an ODI series in the countdown to the World Cup after a disappointing Ashes Test series defeat

Weaknesses

The team isn't anywhere as solid as the previous three editions, primary reason being the quality of replacements of the superstars who graced the 2007 World Cup. Replacing Glenn McGrath, Adam Gilchrist and Matthew Hayden wasn't expected to be easy but the Australian system was always said to plan ahead. The current frontline bowlers are nowhere in that class and skill and the lack of a specialist spinner can be a serious problem. Spinner Jason Krejza made his ODI debut only recently and was a late addition to the squad because of injuries to Nathan Hauritz and Xavier Doherty

BANGLADESH

Shakib Al Hasan (Captain)

Best World Cup performance

Super 8s (2007).

Last World Cup

Super 8s

Captain

Shakib Al Hasan

Coach

Jamie Siddons (Australia)

World Cup win-loss record

Bangladesh 5-14 1 NR

Key Players

Tamim Iqbal, Mohammad Ashraful

Strengths

Once the whipping boys of international cricket, Bangladesh have now unbelievably overtaken the once mighty West Indies and hold eighth place in the current ODI rankings. Their first international was in 1986 and 12 years and 23 matches went by before their maiden win, but they have now beaten almost every team in the ODI version. Bangladesh's first win over an established cricketing nation was against Pakistan at the 1999 World Cup, while in 2005 they famously beat Australia in a ODI in England. More recently, they recorded their first victory against England, their latest two series have seen 4-0 and 3-1 home wins over New Zealand and Zimbabwe respectively. Home conditions will undoubtedly be a major plus, the slow, low pitches suiting their collection of spinners. Dashing opener Tamim Iqbal has emerged as one of the sport's brightest talents – the form book suggests that the Tigers would appear to face a tussle with the West Indies for the fourth place in Group B, with India, England and South Africa expected to qualify

Weaknesses

The Tigers face a tough start at home against co-hosts India and will also miss their fast bowling all-rounder Mashrafe Mortaza, who was left out because of a knee injury. Bangladesh are still among the three teams observers expect to depart from Group B as Al Hasan's boys will need to improve on their two wins recorded in 2007 to advanced to the next stage

CANADA

Ashish Bagai (Captain)

Best World Cup performance

Group Stage (1979, 2003, 2007)

Last World Cup

Group Stage

Captain

Ashish Bagai

Coach

Pubudu Dassanayake (Sri Lanka)

World Cup win-loss record

1-11

Key Players

John Davison, Ashish Bagai

Strengths

Their fourth appearance in the World Cup after finishing runners-up to Ireland in the qualifying tournament. Canada has a talented top-order contributor in John Davison, who made headlines at the 2003 edition with what was then the fastest century in the tournament. The 40-year-old, raised in Australia, smashed 111 off 67 balls in a losing effort against West Indies. He takes his place in the squad despite initially withdrawing over the dropping of Geoff Barnett and Ian Billcliff. Skipper Ashish Bagga and nine other players have roots in Asian and are familiar to the subcontinent conditions

Weaknesses

Overdependence on Davison and Bagai to perform in every match could compound the pressure on the minnows. The lack of depth and experience are the major drawbacks. Canada left out some seasoned veterans in a gamble to promote a handful of younger players into the Cup. Poor form has followed – Canada finished fifth out of six teams in ICC World Cricket League Division I in July 2010, but they twice beat Kenya, the other associate side in their group. A number of one-sided defeat are likely in store, but Canada knows that their mere participation provides the tournament with an important link to cricket's past - their game in the US in 1844 was the first-ever international match

ENGLAND

Andrew Strauss (Captain)

Best World Cup performance

Finalist (1979, 1987, 1992)

Last World Cup

Super 8s

Captain

Andrew Strauss

Coach

Andy Flower (Zimbabwe)

World Cup win-loss record

36-22 1 NR

Key Players

Andrew Strauss, Kevin Pietersen

Strengths

England have reached the finals thrice but never won it so far. The confidence in their ability has been boosted with the World Twenty20 title in the Caribbean in 2010 and five consecutive ODI series wins against South African, Bangladesh (twice), Australia and Pakistan from late 2009 to late 2010.

England has some exceptional players in their lineup – the naturally gifted Pietersen is a true match-winner who can slay any bowling attack; Collingwoods' batting form may be under cloud but the 34-year-old still sets the standard for fielding; and Strauss looks more compact as a batsman and a leader in control. England's search for the crown could end in the subcontinent

Weaknesses

Their recent ODI debacle against Australia (1-6) will rankle no doubt. Further, England has struggled to perform in the subcontinent. Top batsman Eoin Morgan has been lost to injury while Collingwood's woeful form Down Under was the focus of much debate ahead of the World Cup selection. England will have to lift their performance many notches higher if they wish to change their record in the subcontinent

INDIA

Mahendra Singh Dhoni (Captain)

Best World Cup performance

Champions (1983)

Last World Cup

Group Stage

Captain

Mahendra Singh Dhoni

Coach

Gary Kirsten (South Africa)

World Cup win-loss record

32-25, 1 NR

Key Players

Sachin Tendulkar, Sehwag, Harbhajan Singh, Yuvraj Singh, Dhoni

Strengths

Indian should aim for at least a place in the semifinals though nothing less than the trophy will do for their billion fans. They have the world's best batsman, Sachin Tendulkar, who has scored a record number of runs in the World Cup. The explosive Virender Sehwag, Gautam Gambhir, Yuvraj Singh and the astute captain Dhoni make it arguably the most formidable batting lineup in the tournament. To add there is Yusuf Pathan with a rare ability to hit sixes at will – the all-rounder has hit 36 sixes in 45 ODIs. The bowling front will be spearheaded by Zaheer Khan and Harbhajan Singh with the old warhorse Ashish Nehra. To cap it all, they have won 12 of their recent 14 matches at home

Weaknesses

The Indian team has the tendency to crumble under huge expectations at home – every other advantage like familiarity with the conditions and pitch becomes immaterial with the pressure that comes with playing in front of home crowd. The batting lineup can't afford to come crashing in a big-run chase. Too much at stake in a situation where cricket's popularity has increased many times more here than the last time India hosted the tournament

IRELAND

William Porterfield (Captain)

Best World Cup performance

Super 8s (2007)

Last World Cup

Super 8s.

Captain

William Porterfield

Coach

Phil Simmons (West Indies)

World Cup win-loss record

2-6 1 NR.

Key Players

Porterfield, Ed Joyce, Andrew White

Strengths

Ireland are by far the strongest of the Associate nations involved in the tournament. A slot in the quarterfinal is possible – they will be aiming to beat Bangladesh, Netherlands and the West Indies in Group B. The likes of Porterfield, Ed Joyce, the O'Brien brothers and Andrew White have the ability to change matches with devastating knocks. Compared to 2007, when they created a major upset, beating Pakistan in the group stage to reach the Super 8, this time 13 of the 15-man squad are playing professionally, compared with the largely amateur side of four years ago. Seam bowler Boyd Rankin, Ireland's leading wicket-taker at the 2007 event, has recovered from a stress fracture in his foot and Joyce returns to Ireland colours after he was given special dispensation to change his allegiance from England

Weaknesses

Expecting Ireland to edge out any of the full-time ICC team in their group would be a huge upset. The odds are clearly stacked against the Irish who lost three defeats in as many warm-up games in February against New Zealand, Kenya and Zimbabwe, along with a 2-1 loss to Zimbabwe in an ODI series in September at Harare

KENYA

Jimmy Kamande (Captain)

Best World Cup performance

Semifinals (2003)

Last World Cup

Group Stage

Captain

Jimmy Kamande

Coach

Eldine Baptiste (West Indies)

World Cup win-loss record

6-16, 1 tie

Key Players

Thomas Odoyo, Collins Obuya

Strengths

It will be difficult to emulate the achievement of reaching the semifinal of the tournament in 2003, but Kenya still has some experienced campaigners in Steve Tikolo and Thomas Odoyo, both playing their fifth World Cups. Tikolo has played in all the 23 World Cup matches featuring Kenya and has an average of nearly 35 in 129 ODI. Kenya's fielding would be keenly watched in the tournament after using the expertise of the agile South African Jonty Rhodes to improve this department. Skipper Kamande's main job will be to motivate a team that is low on confidence

Weaknesses

Inexperienced with as many as nine World Cup rookies in the side, Kenya have fallen dramatically in recent times. They lost a series of matches to domestic teams in India during a recent tour to acclimatize to subcontinental conditions

THE NETHERLANDS

Peter Borren (Captain)

Best World Cup performance

Group Stage (1996, 2003, 2007)

Last World Cup

Group Stage

Captain

Peter Borren

Coach

Peter Drinnen (Australia)

World Cup win-loss record

2-12

Key Players

Ryan ten Doeschate, Pieter Seelaar

Strengths

Competing in their fourth World Cup, the Dutch have a mixed story that reflects their condition best – their batting is the strongpoint but they are probably the weakest side in the competition. The 27-year-old Peter Borren faces a tough campaign – he is stronger with the ball than the bat. All-rounder Ryan ten Doeschate has played domestic cricket in South Africa, Australia, New Zealand and recently signed up with Kolkata Knight Riders. Doeschate is a big hitter and bowls medium pace. The shock win over hosts England in the 2009 World Twenty20 remains their best moment in international cricket

Weaknesses

Their bowling strength remains a huge suspect and there are no hints that it has improved in the last four years. In the 2007 edition, Herschelle Gibbs created a Cup record by hammering six sixes in one over by Daan van Bunge. It's unlikely that this time the fancied teams will miss the chance to set new batting records against the weak Dutch attack

NEW ZEALAND

Daniel Vettori (Captian)

Best World Cup performance

Semifinals (1975, 1979, 1992, 1999, 2007)

Last World Cup

Semifinals

Captain

Daniel Vettori

Coach

John Wright

World Cup win-loss record

35-26, 1 No Result

Key Players

Vettori, Brendon McCullum, Scott Styris

Strengths

The perennial dark horses of the tournament, the Kiwis appointed former Zealand Test player and India coach John Wright to oversee preparations, which brings huge advantage playing in the subcontinent. Of the seven nations that have played every World Cup, New Zealand are the only one never to have reached the final. The Kiwis rarely succeed without Vettori playing well, and he he has a team of solid all-rounders including the dependable Styris, capable of rising to the occasion. Overall, New Zealand have always performed better in the World Cup tournament in comparison to the longer version

Weaknesses

The Black Caps appear to be the most susceptible team likely to suffer an upset at the hands of the minnows. It's mainly due to the fact that they come into the tournament with only two wins in their last 14 ODIs, including an 11-match losing streak in which it went down 4-0 in Bangladesh and 5-0 in India before winning in the first and last matches of a 3-2 home series loss to Pakistan

PAKISTAN

Shahid Afridi (Captian)

Best World Cup performance

Champions (1992)

Last World Cup

Group Stage

Captain

Shahid Afridi

Coach

Waqar Younis

World Cup win-loss record

30-24, 2 NR.

Key Players

Afridi, Abdul Razzaq, Umar Gul

Strengths

Inconsistencies and unpredictability would mar any team's chance in the World Cup but in the case of Pakistan it acts as a spur to brilliance. Their triumph in the 1992 World Cup after coming whisker close to exit still remains etched in the mind of cricket fans. Even in these bleak moments, they have the lineup to reach the quarterfinals. Paceman Umar Gul is one of the few genuine tearway in the competition with great ability to reverse swing the ball and hurl toe-crushers. Afridi has one of the most envious record in ODI, he along with all-rounder Razzaq can quick turn a match in familiar conditions

Weaknesses

Pakistan's inconsistency is highlighted by the eight wins and eight defeats in their last 16 ODIs. A team with parallel to Mike Tyson's career in individual sport, Pakistan has been in the limelight for all the wrong reasons – fixing controversies and the ban on batsman Salman Butt and frontline pacemen Mohammad Asif and Mohammad Amir, increasing infighting within the team in recent times, feeling wronged on being stripped as one of the co-hosts of the tournament and now depending on an injury-prone Shoaib Akhtar to spearhead the bowling attack. Phew!

SOUTH AFRICA

Graeme Smith (Captian)

Best World Cup performance

Semifinals (1992, 1999, 2007)

Last World Cup

Semifinals

Captain

Graeme Smith

Coach

Corrie van Zyl

World Cup win-loss record

25-13, 2 ties

Key Players

Smith, Jacques Kallis, Dale Steyn

Strengths

Given their form at every World Cup they have participated since 1992 South Africa should have been soaring with confidence. Instead, they are burdened with inexplicable cricket karma. Luckily, the Proteas are used to playing in the subcontinent, have a gritty skipper who brings the same art in facing bowlers, and the indefatigable all-rounder Jacques Kallis is still around and soon expected to be match fit. Kallis has scored 923 runs in 25 World Cup innings at an average of 51, with seven fifties and a top score of 128 not out, plus 16 wickets at a cost of 48 apiece, and is preparing for his fifth World Cup. Givng them support would be Hashim Amla and AB de Villiers, the other two top ODI batsmen in the lineup. Overall, it shouldn't be tough for South Africa to make it to the quarterfinals from a group consisting of India, England, Bangladesh, Ireland and the Netherlands

Weaknesses

To be point-blank, the World Cup jinx. South Africa has a wretched record in the tournament where it has regularly underperformed and could again be troubled by the pressure to win one on the big stage. The bowling department led by Steyn, Morkel, Kallis and Lonwabo Tsotsobe doesn't look as effective as the Proteas are used to on the slower pitches of the subcontinent

SRI LANKA

Kumar Sangakkara (Captian)

Best World Cup performance

Champions (1996)

Last World Cup

Finalist

Captain

Kumar Sangakkara

Coach

Trevor Bayliss (Australia)

World Cup win-loss record

25-30, 1 tie, 1 NR

Key Players

Sangakkara, Muttiah Muralitharan, Tillakaratne Dilshan

Strengths

Till date they remain the only host country to win the World Cup, and they appear to be strong contenders this time too. With players like the consistent Sangakkara, Tillakaratne Dilshan, the inventor of of the infamous "Dilscoop" shot over the wicketkeeper's head and the spinning wizardy of Muttiah Muralitharan, the *doosra* title isn't a far-fetched idea. Sri Lanka also reached the finals in 2007 and have amore consistent record than their other teams from the subcontinent. To add, Muralitharan will be charged up playing his farewell tournament

Weaknesses

The middle order doesn't convey the same formidable assurance it used to earlier. It will only compound pressure on Sangakkara and Muralitharan to win the tournament which their country is co-hosting for the second time. Compared to the last time they won the tournament and 2007 when they reached the final, this time there are fewer match-winners in the team.

WEST INDIES

Darren Sammy *(Captian)*

Best World Cup performance

Champions (1975, 1979)

Last World Cup

Super 8s

Captain

Darren Sammy

Coach

Ottis Gibson

World Cup win-loss record

35-21, 1 NR

Key Players

Chris Gayle, Darren Bravo

Strengths

The once mighty West Indies have taken a drubbing from some of the weakest teams in recent times. That aside, they have one of the most hard-hitting batsman in their lineup. Chris Gayle hit a six so long for Western Australia in a Twenty20 match that a commentator in awe, said: "Anything that travels that far should have a flight attendant". Gayle is the fifth highest six-hitter in ODI and on his day is capable of destroying any attack in the world. If the likes of Chris Gayle, big-hitting Kieron Pollard, Dwayne Bravo and fast bowler Kemar Roach hit their straps at the same time, the West Indies can spring a few suprises!

Weaknesses

Some of the unbelievable stats about the Windies run-up to the World Cup – a 2-0 series defeat by Sri Lanka in January and February followed last year's 5-0 whitewash by South Africa and a 4-0 drubbing in Australia over 2009-2010, though punctuated by a 4-1 win over Zimbabwe. The Caribbeans have not won a ODI against one of the nine other Test-playing nations in 21 matches. Sammy is the fourth captain in as many years, and the team has also been plagued by politicking, lack of funds and a split between the players and board. Remote chances indeed!

ZIMBABWE

Elton Chigumbura (Captain)

Best World Cup performance

Super 6 (1999, 2003)

Last World Cup

Group Stage

Captain

Elton Chigumbura

Coach

Alan Butcher (England)

World Cup win-loss record

8-33 1 tie, 3 NR

Key Players

Chigumbura, Tatenda Taibu

Strengths

The team isn't burdened by the pressure of expectations and has experience in the subcontinental conditions, which suit its spin-oriented bowling attack led by Ray Price and Prosper Utseya. Skipper Chigumbura is likely to be an important presence, while Tatenda Taibu will bring fluent runs and safe hands behind the stumps, having made his 16th ODI fifty in his most recent game in December. It is hard to see the Zimbabweans advance to the quarterfinals ahead of Australia, Pakistan, Sri Lanka or New Zealand in Group A, but if they can beat Kenya and Canada and notch one shock win, it would be enough to make an impact

Weaknesses

There are no Duncan Fletchers or Andy Flowers in the team – their biggest problem. Since the retirement of pacemen Heath Streak and Brandes, Zimbabwe lack a true talisman. The lack of batting depth and bowling department will show against the top teams. Zimbabwe hasn't returned to the form of 1999, when it beat India and South Africa in the World Cup

India's Chances

Imagine the scene, Brazil winning the football World Cup at Rio, an Englishman clinching the grass court title at Wimbledon, or closer home India lifting the cricket World Cup in the subcontinent. Today, Australia isn't the same force as it used to be a couple of years back, South Africa, Pakistan and Sri Lanka have played superbly in patches but fallen to inconsistencies and incongruous situations. In the last four years India alone has displayed the hunger to improve from match to match, and quite unusual by its own standard, followed a method to the 2011 World Cup. From being knocked out in the group stage in the previous edition, India has improved tremendously in all forms of the game – winning the inaugural T20 World Cup, soaring in the Test and ODI rankings and their stars shining brighter with every outing.

What also makes India the hot favourites for the tournament is that most cricket fans across the world look forward to watching Sachin Tendulkar for the longest TV-time. Not suprising therefore that TRPs are being calculated for the duration Tendulkar occupies the crease. He is India's greatest match-winning ODI player, has scored a record number of runs in the World Cup in addition to owning some of the most prestigious records in batting in Test and ODIs.

It might be a bit premature to aver that there are similarities between the team of 1983 and 2011 before a ball has been bowled, but the uncanny coincidence can't be denied. Both teams have several players with match-winning ability in their ranks, right up to the relatively unknown spinner Piyush Chawla (remember the then unknown Kirti Azad tightening the lease on England in the '83 semis) as seen in the warmup games. Unlike the campaign in 1996 and 2003 where the Indians depended on a couple of stars to deliver, the 2011 squad presents a more assuring picture as far as match-winners are concerned. Besides, the current Indian team has the most dynamic batting side in the tournament – Tendulkar, Virender Sehwag, Gautam Gambhir, Virat Kohli, Yuvraj Singh, Dhoni, Yusuf Pathan and Suresh Raina. This is arguably India's strongest World Cup batting lineup with clear-cut emphasis on making an impact rather than just accumulating runs.

The bowling options appear limited in comparison, but they have come to the rescue on many occasions when the more-famous batting order has crumbled to pressure. "Bhajji" and Zaheer Khan have the experience of turning matches on their heads against almost all the major teams, and they will be supported by the likes of Ashish Nehra, Sreesanth, Chawla, Munaf Patel and Ravichandran Ashwin.

This Indian team has the potential of becoming a world champion and reigning at the top for a long time. They can't afford to be bogged down by pressure, specially the home kind. There was a long time when the Indian teams didn't perform away, and now it seems playing in front of the home crowd can be a bogey – these are surmountable challenges for a team backed by more than a billion fans. Come April 2 at the Wankhede, the answer will be known!

Team India

Know Your Stars

Captain Cool

	M	NO	Runs	HS	SR	Ave	50	100	6s	4s
WC	3	0	29	29	100	9.66	0	0	1	2
ODIs	177	39	5808	183*	87.8	48.8	37	7	119	446

MS Dhoni

There is something special about Dhoni which is undefined so far – commentators describe him as the best thing to happen to Indian cricket after Tendulkar. It is perhaps the streak of wins that India has enjoyed under him, the rankings in the ODI and Test simultaneously, a captain not tempestuous in the dressing room, and tolerant of quirks of both genius and wayward players than ever before. The flamboyant 'MSD' has led India to its first-ever ODI series wins in Sri Lanka and New Zealand, the won the inaugural World Twenty20 and the No.1 ranking in Test cricket. Dhoni's exploits with the bat and wicket-keeping has been consistent since he made his debut n 2004. His unbeaten 183 off 145 balls against Sri Lanka in Jaipur, 2005, is still the highest score made by any batsman in a chase, and he is also the youngest wicketkeeper-batsman to complete the double of scoring 4,000 runs and 100 dismissals. An advertising favourite, Dhoni's astute leadership and sensible batting will be under tremendous pressure.

Run Machine

	M	NO	Runs	HS	SR	Ave	50	100	6s	4s
W C	36	4	1796	152	88.21	57.93	13	4	19	189
ODIs	444	41	17629	200*	86.18	44.97	93	46	18	1929

Sachin Ramesh Tendulakar

The only batsman to score a double century, the first one to cross 11,000 runs in ODIs, holder of the maximum runs record in World Cup, 60 times man of the match award in ODIs, 14 times man of the series in ODI tournaments, and more than a dozen endorsement contracts – winning the World Cup is probably the only major milestone missing in Tendulkar's wishlist. After more than two decades of being the run machine, analyzing his strengths and weaknesses if any, would be injustice. His personal records in the five World Cup barring for 2007 and 1992 editions have been outstanding, and he still remains the power centre of Indian cricket. Like all great players, Tendulkar is the source of inspiration for his young team and he has the added calibre of making things happen with the ball in case one of the front bowler hits a bad patch. It is unfair to speculate whether this is indeed going to be Tendulkar's swansong at the World Cup but this will definitely be the best time for him to try to win the Cup.

Modern Zen Master

	M	NO	Runs	HS	SR	Ave	50	100	6s	4s
W C	14	0	463	114	95.66	33.07	2	1	11	59
ODIs	228	9	7380	146	103.27	34.64	36	13	121	1019

Virender Sehwag

His strike rate–second in the world to Pakistan's Shahid Afridi–makes him one of the most dangerous batsman in the world. "Viru" made his debut in ODI in 1999 and it wasn't until 2001 when he was promoted to open the innings that he found his career breakthrough and scored a century off just 69 balls against New Zealand. Since then Viru has come to relish the Kiwi attack and he notched the record of scoring the fastest century by an Indian, off 60 balls in 2009. Seven out of his 14 ODI centuries have come while chasing. The opener has earned quite a few titles, 'Sultan of Multan', the 'Cricket's modern Zen master' etc. The 2011 Cup will be a chance for him to turnaround his record. He had a mediocre outing in 2003, scoring 299 runs, and an unforgettable 2007 Cup except a century against minnows Bermuda. Ironically, it is Sehwag's explosive knocks in Test matches, the two 300s, which frighten his opponents the most. To date, the opener has 20 man of the match awards in ODIs to his credit, and India will be looking up to him to provide a rousing start.

Man for all occasions

Gautam Gambhir

The quiet Gambhir can switch his style according to the situation, though he is best at anchoring the side during a chase. His presence is a great strength to the batting if any of the opener returns early to the pavilion. He is the best man to stall an attack. He faced the disappointment of being dropped from the 2007 edition, and will obviously be raring to go all out this time.

	M	NO	Runs	HS	SR	Ave	50	100	6s	4s
ODIs	105	10	3680	150*	86.52	40.43	21	9	16	411

World Cup Debut

Hardest Hitter of sixes

	M	NO	Runs	HS	SR	Ave	50	100	6s	4s
W C	14	3	376	83	94.71	37.6	3	0	10	29
ODIs	265	34	7689	139	87.65	36.61	45	12	141	788

Yuvraj Singh

The 29-year-old dashing all-rounder has produced some stupendous knocks in the past and not surprisingly is considered India's greatest match-winning batsman in ODI after Tendulkar. It started right from his debut tournament when he clobbered against a quality Aussie attack in 2000. His performance has dipped in recent times but players like Yuvraj relish the big-stage challenge. The star of India's World T20 title, Yuvraj is looking for the biggest prize.

Run hungary

	M	NO	Runs	HS	SR	Ave	50	100	6s	4s
ODIs	45	6	1672	118	82.12	46.44	12	4	11	162

Virat Kohli

Extremely cool under pressure, Kohli is an attacking batsman with an impressive batting record in the condensed version. The 22-year-old is also one of the best fielders in the current squad along with Yuvraj Singh and Suresh Raina. The second Indian skipper to bring home the Under-22 World Cup, KohIi made his debut in 2008 and has a reputation for being run-hungry in the middle and attempts to convert his 50s into a big score.

World Cup Debut

Raina haina!

	M	NO	Runs	HS	SR	Ave	50	100	6s	4s
ODIs	111	18	2639	116*	89.6	35.18	16	3	57	225

Suresh Raina

The attacking Kashmiri left-hander is probably the best fielder in the team after Yuvraj Singh. The 24-year-old Raina is an asset when it comes to handling pressure but he has to get his response quicker against short-pitch delivery. His ability to hit the stumps from the infield makes him a player difficult to ignore.

World Cup Debut

Bowlers' nightmare

	M	NO	Runs	HS	SR	Ave	50	100	6s	4s	Wkts.
ODIs	45	10	694	123*	115.09	33.04	3	2	36	55	30

Yusuf Pathan

His reputation as a match-winner has grown dramatically after the IPL and the recent ODI series against New Zealand. Pathan has the second best strike rate in the team after Sehwag and he can handle pressure superbly too. The all-rounder who bats in the lower mid-order has a penchant to hit sixes almost at will. Pathan's blazing 123 not out helped India chase New Zealand's 315 at Bangalore in December 2010. It is a timely entry for Indian team–a lower middle-order batsman who can put the opposition into disarray in the slog overs.

World Cup Debut

Turbanator on the roll

	M	NO	Runs	HS	SR	Ave	50	100	6s	4s	Wkts.
W C	12	3	75	28	91.46	15	0	0	3	6	11
ODIs	217	32	1125	49	81.58	13.23	0	0	32	86	246

Harbhajan Singh

India's bowling spearhead has 242 wickets in the shorter version and can be a dangerous lower order bat too. Like his Punjab team-mate Yuvraj Singh, the "Turbanator" relishes the challenge of raising his game against tough teams. After his fairytale comeback in 2001 against Australia, the off-spinner needs another outstanding tournament on his CV. The World Cup is the biggest opportunity to leave his mark.

Getting better with age

	M	NO	Runs	HS	SR	Ave	50	100	6s	4s	Wkts.
W C	14	2	34	15*	69.38	6.8	0	0	0	4	23
ODIs	182	35	763	34*	73.22	12.71	0	0	24	65	252

Zaheer Khan

Looking more dangerous than ever in his new avatar since he made his debut in 2000, Zaheer Khan will spearhead the Indian pace attack. The good thing is he is one Indian pacer who uses the local condition to his advantage and is unafraid of varying his swing and pace to attack the bowler. Pressure will be on Zaheer and Harbhajan to perform consistently in order to avoid wearing out the other – they were effective together against South Africa recently.

From speedster to Mr Accurate

	M	NO	Runs	HS	SR	Ave	50	100	6s	4s	Wkts.
W C	3	0	25	15	78.12	12.5	0	0	0	3	4
ODIs	54	14	73	15	66.97	8.11	0	0	1	7	65

Munaf Patel

The Baroda lad has changed track from being an express bowler to professing economy and accuracy. His performance in South Africa is a pointer that Patel's hunger for wickets has not waned despite the curb on speed. He skittled out four Proteas batsmen to script a one-run victory for India in the second ODI in Johannesburg. It is a good omen for India that Patel is looking dangerous.

IPL Impact - He is Back

	M	NO	Runs	HS	SR	Ave	50	100	6s	4s	Wkts.
W C	9	1	8	8*	200	-	0	0	0	2	15
ODIs	117	21	140	24	58.09	6.08	0	0	3	12	154

Ashish Nehra

His career-best figure of 6 for 23 against England in the 2003 World Cup is still fresh in the memory, but his career has been marred by several injuries. Nehra made his comeback into international cricket after a gap of four years and his successful outing in the IPL. His experience could be a vital support for Zaheer and Harbhajan in the death overs.

	M	NO	Runs	HS	SR	Ave	50	100	6s	4s	Wkts.
ODIs	22	5	36	13*	66.66	6	0	0	0	3	28

Piyush Chawla

At 17, he made headlines when he bowled Sachin Tendulkar with a googly in a Challenger series match. The surprise pick of the Indian team has shut his critics with good shows in the warmup games, but Chawla needs to prove himself early in the tournament. The 22-year-old leg-spinner has good control and variation but needs to come up with special effort to get his legbreak right consistently.

World Cup Debut

Quirky Sensation

	M	NO	Runs	HS	SR	Ave	50	100	6s	4s	Wkts.
ODIs	51	10	44	10*	36.36	4	0	0	0	2	75

S Sreesanth

A replacement for the injured Praveen Kumar in the side, Sreesanth is not really considered ideal for Indian conditions, but he has a knack for taking quick wickets. The 'dancing sensation' has bagged 75 wickets in 51 ODIs, a career-best of six for 55 in an inning. His problem with discipline has hit the headlines more than his performance recently, and that is what he needs to check to ensure a memorable World Cup.

World Cup Debut

IPL Star on test

	M	NO	Runs	HS	SR	Ave	50	100	6s	4s	Wkts.
ODIs	7	0	38	38	111.76	19	0	0	1	4	14

R Ashwin

Ashwin's exploits with the Chennai Super Kings in the IPL got him noticed for the 2011 World Cup. The 24-year-old right-hander and off-break bowler made his ODI debut against Sri Lanka in 2010. The youngster smashed four boundaries and one mighty sixer to score 38 off 32 balls in a lost cause, but his temperament at the highest level earned him praises. Also known for his ability to bowl the "carom ball", Ashwin is studying to be an engineer. He can use the World Cup to build bridges for his cricketing future.

World Cup Debut

Venues

India
Sri Lanka
Bangladesh

It was unthinkable 28 years back that one of the most conservative sports body would allow the game to travel outside the confines of one country and help it to expand, right up to Chittagong. For those who complain that cricket is a game played by merely "10 countries", it's time to acknowledge that at least something good is being done, apart from the cricket obviously. The world governing body for football, FIFA, or IAAF (athletics) or much closer the FIH (international hockey federation) have struggled to develop the game outside the existing power centres, but cricket's face is changing constantly. From England and Australia holding the baton in the first phase to India and Pakistan in the second phase, and probably Bangladesh and Scotland will be the carriers in the immediate future. One of the biggest benefits of hosting the 2011 World Cup in the subcontinent for the third time in less than 25 years, is that it has given a new identity to the poor and cyclone-ravaged Bangladesh.

The 2011 tournament appears more organised than the previous two editions held in the subcontinent barring for the initial fiasco with Pakistan being stripped from co-hosting matches due to security concerns. After the re-allocation of matches originally intended to be played in Pakistan, India will now host 29 matches across eight venues including the final and one semi-final, Sri Lanka will host 12 in three venues, including one semifinal while Bangladesh will stage 8 at two venues as well as the opening ceremony on February 17. The first match gets underway on February 19 between co-hosts India and Bangaldesh at the Sher-e-Bangla National Stadium in Mirpur,

Dhaka, and the finals will be held at Mumbai's Wankhede Stadium on April 2. We look at all the host venues in details later in this segment.

As far as the format is concerned, this edition uses the same format as the last time it was held in the subcontinent. The only change being the increase in the number of participating teams increased from 12 to 14. The first round of the tournament will be a round-robin league in which the 14 teams are divided into two groups of seven teams each. The seven teams play each other once with the Top-4 from each group qualifying for the quarterfinals. The format ensures that each team gets to play a minimum of six matches even if they fail to make it to the quarterfinals.

Stumpy, a cute elephant, is the official mascot of the tenth edition of the World Cup.

India

1. Eden Gardens, Kolkata. Capacity 82,000

The second biggest cricket stadium in the world behind the MCG in Australia, Eden Gardens is expected to hold 82,000 people following renovations for the 2011 World Cup. Prior to the 1987 World Cup, the capacity was said to be around 130,000. The stadium which was established in 1864, is also the home of Kolkata Knight Riders in the Indian Premier League (IPL). It has also hosted the finals of the 1987 World Cup.

2. MA Chidambaram Stadium, Chennai. Capacity 50,000

Commonly known as the Chepauk, the venue has witnessed several cricketing heights being achieved on its ground and a tradition of housing sporting crowds. The first match was played here in 1934, India won its first Test match here in 1952 versus England, and the venue has hosted a tied Test between India and Australia – only th4 second instance in the history of the game. The MACS is also the the IPL home ground of Chennai Super Kings, the adopted team of Indian captain MS Dhoni.

3. Feroz Shah Kotla, New Delhi. Capacity 48,000

Named after the famous Delhi Sultan who ruled in the 14th century, the Kotla's best cricking memories were scripted by India's ace leg-spinner Anil Kumble who bagged all 10 wickets in an innings against Pakistan at this venue in 1999 – only the second time in the history of the game. That apart, Kotla is also the home ground of the Delhi Daredevils in the IPL and the leading nursery for several decades.

4. Vidarbha Cricket Association Stadium, Nagpur. Capacity 45,000

A relatively new stadium, it hosted its first international match between India and Australia in 2008. India won the match by 172 runs and the spinners from both teams had a feast. Harbhajan Singh, who bagged seven wickets in that Test and Indian skipper MS Dhoni who slammed a century against Australia in an ODI in 2009-10 will have good memories of this venue.

5. Sardar Patel Stadium, Ahmedabad. Capacity 50,000

The Motera has witnessed many milestones being achieved in the game despite being a relatively new venue. Two Indian legends – Sunil Gavaskar and Kapil Dev reached the 10,000-run mark and 432-wicket in Test cricket respectively here. The stadium has hosted more ODI games than probably any venue in India with the exception of the Eden Gardens in recent times.

6. Wankhede Stadium, Mumbai. Capacity 45,000

In terms of number of years the Wankhede has been around for just 36 years, but this is the place where cricketers are worshipped, right from the names of the stands, gates and pavilion, to the milestones – international or first-class– recorded on the field. To give an example, former Indian captain Ravi Shastri's six sixes off an over in the fastest double century scored in a first-class game was played at the Wankhede.

7. Punjab Cricket Association Stadium, Mohali. Capacity 35,000

One of the youngest stadiums in India, the Mohali stadium boasts of a lush outfield and a lively pitch for quickies. It hosted its first ODI between India and South Africa in 1993, and the first Test was played here in the following years between India and West Indies. The stadium is also the home ground of the Kings Eleven Punjab in the IPL.

8. M Chinnaswamy Stadium, Bangalore. Capacity 42,000

The Chinnaswamy has witnessed some of the most intense games in recent times – India vs Pakistan clash in the 1996 World Cup remains an all-time favourite for many cricket aficionado. The stadium hosted its first ODI in 1982 with India beating Sri Lanka by six wickets. The stadium is also the home ground of Royal Challengers in the IPL and hosts India's National Cricket Academy.

Sri Lanka & Bangladesh

1. R Premadasa Stadium, Colombo. Capacity 35,000

Runs rain here on this ground. Sri Lanka amassed 952 for six against India in 1997-98 series, which is the highest score for a Test innings. The Premadas is one of the main stadiums for the tournament and it has undergone a lot of renovations. The venue will host seven matches.

2. Muttiah Muralitharan Int Stadium, Kandy. Capacity 35,000

Named in honour of the ace Lankan spinner, the Kandy stadium is the newest stadium and will make its ODI debut in the 2011 World Cup. Three matches are scheduled to take place here with Pakistan featuring in two of them. The MMIC stadium is the eighth cricket stadium to be built in Sri Lanka.

3. Mahinda Rajapaksa Stadium, Hambantota. Capacity 35,000

Another new stadium constructed specially to host the World Cup, the Rajapaksa stadium will host two games involving two leading contenders against the minnows. The first ODI match gets underway between Sri Lanka and Canada on February 20 while Pakistan takes on Kenya three days later.

5. Chittagong Divisional Stadium, Chittagong. Capacity 20,000

Located in south-east Bangladesh, bordering the north-eastern states of India, the Chittagong Stadium became an international venue in 2007 – the first Test featured the host and Sri Lanka. The stadium will host several day-night matches in the tournament including England vs Bangladesh on March 11 and Bangladesh vs Netherland on March 14.

6. Shere Bangla National Stadium, Mirpur, Dhaka. Capacity 25,000

Names after their freedom fighter, AK Fazlul Haque, the stadium located just outside the capital hosted its first ODI match when Bangladesh played Zimbabwe in 2006. The ground will host four crucial games involving Bangladesh, starting the one against India in the inaugural on February 19, and Ireland, West Indies and England.

Umpires 2011

The World Cup has seen some legendary decision-makers in the middle, from Dickie Bird to David Shepherd and more recently Steve Bucknor. For the 10th edition, the ICC has selected a total of 18 umpires excluding a reserve umpire. The list includes 5 from Australia, 6 from Asia, 3 from England, 2 from New Zealand and 1 each from South Africa and West Indies. The following are the names of the 18 umpires officiating at the tournament

Australia

Simon Taufel, Steve Davis, Rod Tucker, Daryl Harper, Bruce Oxenford.

England

Ian Gould, Richard Kettleborough, Nigel Llong.

India

Shavir Tarapore, Amiesh Saheba.

New Zealand

Billy Bowden, Tony Hill.

Pakistan

Aleem Dar, Asad Rauf.

South Africa

Marais Erasmus.

Sri Lanka

Asoka de Silva, Kumar Dharmasena.

West Indies

Billy Doctrove.

Funny Shots

Different Strokes

Dilliscoop, Helicopter shots and many more

The most traditional sport has never been allergic to innovations on the highest stage, though sometimes they've been down right silly ones. Over the years the World Cup tournaments has seen several unusual ploys and unconventional methods that players use to outsmart each other – the under-arm bowling tactics (1983) or launching the attack through a spinner and introducing the concept of pinch hitters like Kiwi Mark Greatbatch (1992) and Sri Lankan Sanath Jayasuriya (1996). The unusual methods applied with the bat to stupefy the bowlers and fielders has proved to be quite effective — some of these are Indian skipper MS Dhoni's 'Helicopter shot', Sri Lankan Tillakaratne Dilshan's 'Diliscoop', Englishman Kevin Pietersen's 'Switch Shot' , Zimbabwean Douglas Marillier's 'Ramp shot' or the ones which have been around longer like the 'Paddle Sweep', 'Slog Shot', 'Upper Cut', 'Reverse Sweep'. Here is a look at the four unusual ones in recent times:

Dilscoop shot

A product of Twenty20 cricket, it is attributed to Sri Lankan right-handed batsman Tillakaratne Dilshan who discovered the shot against England in the 2009 World T20. The stroke is produced as the batsman goes on one knee to a good length or slightly short of length ball off a fast or medium paced bowler, and scoops the ball over the head of the 'keeper. The ball travels like lightening to the ropes.

Helicopter shot

The shot hasn't been executed by its 'inventor', Indian captain MS Dhoni for quite some time, but a TV campaign has managed to stir up interest before the WC. This is how the shot is executed: As soon as the ball touches the pitch, it is hit with the bat immediately just like hitting with a broom. The bat rotates in the fashion of a helicopter, and hence the name.

Switch shot

England's star batsman Kevin Pietersen introduced this shot. Its basically about changing the stance in the midst of a delivery. When bowler is bowling the ball, the batsman changes the stance and hits the ball. For instance, a right-hander will change to left hander and strike the ball to put the fielders in complete disarray. Pietersen tried this switch shot for the first time against Sri Lanka's ace spinner Muttaiah Muralitharan in 2006.

Ramp shot

Douglas Marillier used this shot to great effect in an ODI against India in 2002. The Zimbabwean scored an unbeaten 56 and outsmarted Zaheer Khan for his team's victory. The bat is used as a ramp to flick the ball high and hard over the wicket-keeper for a boundary. It's a risky and unorthodox shot, somewhat similar to Diliscoop. India's Robin Uthappa and England's Paul Collingwood have used this shot frequently in IPL.

Watch this space for more unconventional shots to be pioneered in the 2011 edition!

Schedule 2011

DATE	TIME	MATCH	VENUE	COUNTRY
19-Feb-11	14:30	Group B : Bangladesh vs India, 1st ODI	Dhaka	BANGLADESH
20-Feb-11	09:30	Group A : New Zealand vs Kenya, 2nd ODI	Chennai	INDIA
20-Feb-11	14:30	Group A : Sri Lanka vs Canada, 3rd ODI	Hambantota	SRILANKA
21-Feb-11	14:30	Group A : Australia vs Zimbabwe, 4th ODI	Ahmedabad	INDIA
22-Feb-11	14:30	Group B : England vs Netherlands, 5th ODI	Nagpur	INDIA
23-Feb-11	14:30	Group A : Pakistan vs Kenya, 6th ODI	Hambantota	SRILANKA
24-Feb-11	14:30	Group B : South Africa vs West Indies, 7th ODI	Delhi	INDIA
25-Feb-11	09:30	Group B : Bangladesh vs Ireland, 8th ODI	Dhaka	BANGLADESH
25-Feb-11	14:30	Group A : Australia vs New Zealand, 9th ODI	Nagpur	INDIA
26-Feb-11	14:30	Group A : Pakistan vs Sri Lanka, 10th ODI	Colombo	SRILANKA
27-Feb-11	14:30	Group B : India vs England, 11th ODI	Bangalore	INDIA
28-Feb-11	09:30	Group A : Canada vs Zimbabwe, 12th ODI	Nagpur	INDIA
28-Feb-11	14:30	Group B : West Indies vs Netherlands, 13th ODI	Delhi	INDIA
01-Mar-11	14:30	Group A : Sri Lanka vs Kenya, 14th ODI	Colombo	SRILANKA
02-Mar-11	14:30	Group B : England vs Ireland, 15th ODI	Bangalore	INDIA
03-Mar-11	09:30	Group B : South Africa vs Netherlands, 16th ODI	Mohali	INDIA
03-Mar-11	14:30	Group A : Pakistan vs Canada, 17th ODI	Colombo	SRILANKA
04-Mar-11	09:30	Group A : New Zealand vs Zimbabwe, 18th ODI	Ahmedabad	INDIA
04-Mar-11	14:30	Group B : Bangladesh vs West Indies, 19th ODI	Dhaka	BANGLADESH
05-Mar-11	14:30	Group A : Australia vs Sri Lanka, 20th ODI	Colombo	SRILANKA

DATE	TIME	MATCH	VENUE	COUNTRY
06-Mar-11	09:30	Group B : South Africa vs England, 21st ODI	Chennai	INDIA
06-Mar-11	14:30	Group B : India vs Ireland, 22nd ODI	Bangalore	INDIA
07-Mar-11	14:30	Group A : Canada vs Kenya, 23rd ODI	Delhi	INDIA
08-Mar-11	14:30	Group A : Pakistan vs New Zealand, 24th ODI	Kandy	SRILANKA
09-Mar-11	14:30	Group B : India vs Netherlands, 25th ODI	Delhi	INDIA
10-Mar-11	14:30	Group A : Sri Lanka vs Zimbabwe, 26th ODI	Kandy	SRILANKA
11-Mar-11	09:30	Group B : West Indies vs Ireland, 27th ODI	Mohali	INDIA
11-Mar-11	14:30	Group B : Bangladesh vs England, 28th ODI	Chittagong	BANGLADESH
12-Mar-11	14:30	Group B : India vs South Africa, 29th ODI	Nagpur	INDIA
13-Mar-11	09:30	Group A : New Zealand vs Canada, 30th ODI	Mumbai	INDIA
13-Mar-11	14:30	Group A : Australia vs Kenya, 31st ODI	Bangalore	INDIA
14-Mar-11	09:30	Group B : Bangladesh vs Netherlands, 32nd ODI	Chittagong	BANGLADESH
14-Mar-11	14:30	Group A : Pakistan vs Zimbabwe, 33rd ODI	Kandy	SRILANKA
15-Mar-11	14:30	Group B : South Africa vs Ireland, 34th ODI	Kolkata	INDIA
16-Mar-11	14:30	Group A : Australia vs Canada, 35th ODI	Bangalore	INDIA
17-Mar-11	14:30	Group B : England vs West Indies, 36th ODI	Chennai	INDIA
18-Mar-11	09:30	Group A : Ireland vs Netherlands, 37th ODI	Kolkata	INDIA
18-Mar-11	14:30	Group A : Sri Lanka vs New Zealand, 38th ODI	Mumbai	INDIA
19-Mar-11	09:30	Group B : Bangladesh vs South Africa, 39th ODI	Dhaka	BANGLADESH
19-Mar-11	14:30	Group A : Pakistan vs Australia, 40th ODI	Colombo	SRILANKA
20-Mar-11	09:30	Group A : Zimbabwe vs Kenya, 41st ODI	Kolkata	INDIA
20-Mar-11	14:30	Group B : India vs West Indies, 42nd ODI	Chennai	INDIA

Guess the Qtr. Finalists...

GROUP A

CN	AUS	PAK	NZ	SL	ZIM	CAN	KEN	PTS	RANK*
AUS									
PAK									
NZ									
SL									
ZIM									
CAN									
KEN									

*Based on their performance the FOUR best teams will be rated A-1,A-2,A-3,A-4

GROUP B

CN	IND	SA	ENG	WI	BAN	IRE	NED	PTS	RANK*
IND									
SA									
ENG									
WI									
BAN									
IRE									
NED									

*Based on their performance the FOUR best teams will be rated B-1,B-2,B-3,B-4

...and the Winner

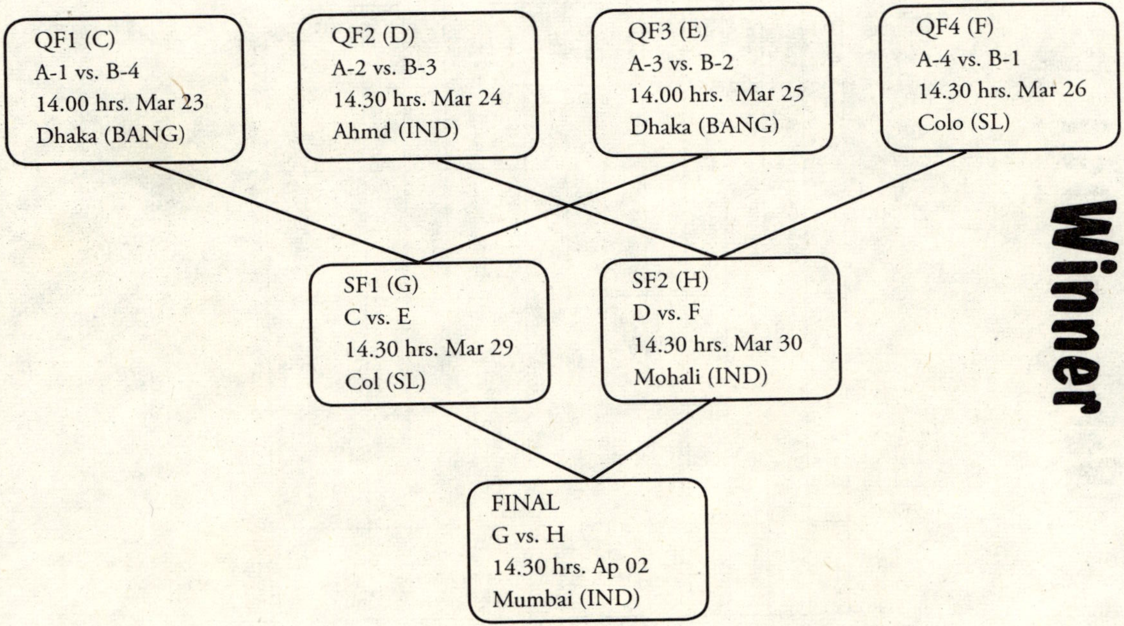

Results

Warm-up 2011

Date	Country A	Country B	Venue	Winning team	Won by
12 Feb.2011	NZ 311	IRE 279 in 48.2 ovr	Nagpur(IND)	**NZ**	32 runs
12 Feb.2011	ZIM 152 in 41.5 ovr	SA 153 in 23.3 ovr	Chennai(IND)	**SA**	8 wkts 159 balls
12 Feb.2011	WI 253	KEN 192 in 45.3 ovr	Colombo(SL)	**WL**	61 runs
12 Feb.2011	SL 351	NETH 195 in 47.3 ovr	Pallekele(SL)	**SL**	156 runs
12 Feb.2011	BANG 113 in 19.2 ovr	CAN 112 in 37.3 ovr	Chittagong(BANG)	**BANG**	9 wkts 184 balls
13 Feb.2011	IND 214 in 44.3 ovr	AUS 176 in 37.5 ovr	Bangalore(IND)	**IND**	38 runs
15 Feb.2011	AUS 217 47.1 ovr	SA 218 in 44.2 ovr	Bangalore(IND)	**SA**	7 wkt 34 balls
15 Feb.2011	IRE 245 in 49.3 ovr	ZIM 244 all out	Nagpur(IND)	**IRE**	4 wkts 3-balls
15 Feb.2011	KEN 263 all out	NETH 264 in 49.1 ovr	Pallekele(SL)	**NETH**	2 wkts 5-balls
15 Feb.2011	BANG 196 in 41.4 ovr	PAK 285 all out	Dhaka(BANG)	**PAK**	89 runs
15 Feb.2011	SL 282 in 47.3 ove	WI 281 all out	Colombo(SL)	**SL**	4 wkt 15 balls
16 Feb.2011	IND 360/5 in 50 ovr	NZ 243 all out in 43.1 ovr	Chennai(IND)	**IND**	117 runs
16 Feb.2011	ENG 243 in 49.4 ovr	CAN 227 in 46.1 ovr	DHAKA (BANG)	**ENG**	16 runs
18 Feb. 2011	ENG 273 in 49.4 ovr	PAK 206 in 46.1 Ovr	Fatullah (BANG)	ENG	69 runs

Statsplay

Records are meant to be broken. Watch out...

Highest individual runs

Runs	Player	Match	Place	Year
188*	Gary Kirsten	SA v UAE	Rawalpindi	1996
183	Sourav Ganguly	IND v SL	Taunton	1999
181	Vivian Richards	WI v SL	Karachi	1987
175*	Kapil Dev	IND v ZIM	Tunbridge Wells	1983
172*	Craig Wishart	ZIM v NAM	Harare	2003
171*	Glenn Turner	NZ v EA	Birmingham	1975
160	Imran Nazir	PAK v ZIM	Kingston	2007
158	Matthew Hayden	AUS v WI	North Sound	2007
161	Andrew Hudson	SA v HOL	Rawalpindi	1996
152	Sachin Tendulkar	IND v NAM	Pietermaritzberg	2003

Centuries in the opening match from 1975 to 2007

Year	Runs	Player	Match	Place
1975	171	Glenn Turner	NZ v EA	Birmingham
1975	137	Dennis Amiss	ENG v IND	Lord's
1979	106	Gordon Greenidge	WI v IND	Birmingham
1983	102	Allan Lamb	ENG v NZ	The Oval
1987	103	Javed Miandad	PAK v SL	Hyderabad(Pak)
1992	100	Martin Crowe	NZ v AUS	Auckland
1992	100	David Boon	AUS v NZ	Auckland
1996	101	Nathan Astle	NZ v ENG	Ahmedabad
1999		Nil		
2003	116	Brian Lara	WI v SA	Cape Town
2007		Nil		

Centurions on debut

RUNS	Player	Match	Place	Year
171*	Glenn Turner	NZ v EA	Birmingham	1975
137	Dennis Amiss	ENG v IND	Lord's	1975
102	Allan Lamb	ENG v NZ	The Oval	1983
110	Trevor Chappell	AUS v IND	Nottingham	1983
110	Geoff Marsh	AUS v IND	Madras	1987
115*	Andy Flower	ZIM v SL	New Plymouth	1992
101	Nathan Astle	NZ v ENG	Ahmedabad	1996
188	Gary Kirsten	SA v UAE	Rawalpindi	1996
172	Craig Wishart	ZIM v NAM	Harare	2003
141	Scott Styris	NZ v SL	Bloemfontein	2003
143	Andrew Symonds	AUS v PAK	Johannesburg	2003
115	Jeremy Bray	IR v ZIM	Kingston	2007

Top 10 batting strike rate

Strike Rate	Players	Match played	Highest	100s	50s	Average
121.17	Lance Klusener	14	57	-	3	124.00
115.84	John Davison	9	111	1	2	34.11
115.15	Kapil Dev	29	175*	1	1	37.16
100.81	A De Villiers	10	146	1	2	37.20
100.70	Wasim Akram	38	43	-	-	19.36
98.01	Adam Gilchrist	31	149	1	8	36.16
95.66	Virender Sehwag	14	114	1	2	33.07
94.98	Michael Clarke	11	93*	-	4	87.20
94.71	Yuvraj Singh	14	83	-	3	37.20
94.07	Mark Boucher	25	75*	-	2	27.21

10 superfast 100s

Balls	Player	Match	Place	Year
66	Matthew Hayden	AUS v SA	Basseterre	2007
67	John Davison	CAN v WI	Centurion	2003
72	Adam Gilchrist	AUS v SL	Bridgetown	2007
81	Virender Sehwag	IND v BER	Port of Spain	2007
82	Clive Lloyd	WI v AUS	Lord's	1975
82	Brad Hodge	AUS v HOL	Basseterre	2007
83	Brian Lara	WI v SA	Karachi	1996
84	Sachin tendulkar	IND v KEN	Bristol	1999
85	Sunil Gavaskar	IND v NZ	Nagpur	1987
85	Ricky Ponting	AUS v SCL	Basseterre	2007

10 superfast 50s

Balls	Player	Match	Place	Year
20	Brendon McCullum	NZ v CAN	Gros Islet	2007
21	Mark Boucher	SA v HOL	Basseterre	2007
22	Mark Boucher	SA v WI	St George's	2007
23	Brian Lara	WI v CAN	Centurion	2003
23	John Davison	CAN v NZ	Gros Islet	2007
24	Wavell Hinds	WI v CAN	Centurian	2003
25	Andy Blignaut	ZIM v AUS	Bulawayo	2003
25	John Davison	CAN v NZ	Benoni	2003
26	Sachin Tendulkar	IND v BER	Port of spain	2007
28	Tom Moody	AUS v BAN	Chester-Le-Street	1999

Youngest centuries

At the Age of	Player	RUNS	Match	Year
21 years, 76 days	Ricky Ponting	102	AUS v WI	1996
22 years, 300 days	Sachin Tendulkar	127*	IND v KEN	1996
23 years, 301 days	Andy Flower	115	ZIM v SL	1992

Year-wise Highest Runs Average in the World Cup

World Cup Year	Players	Match played	High-est	100s	50s	Total Runs	Aver-age
1975	Glenn Turner	4	171*	2	-	333	166.50
1979	Gorden Greenidge	4	106*	1	2	253	84.33
1983	David Gower	7	130	1	1	384	76.80
1987	Graham Gooch	8	115	1	3	471	58.87
1992	Martin Crowe	9	100*	1	4	456	114.00
1996	Sachin Tendulkar	7	137	2	3	523	87.16
1999	Rahul Dravid	8	145	2	3	461	65.85
2003	Sachin Tendulkar	11	152	1	6	673	61.18
2007	Matthew Hayden	11	158	3	1	659	73.22

Record partnership for each wicket

Wicket No.	Runs	Between Players	Match played	Place	Year
1	194	Saeed Anwar & Wajahatullah Wasti	PAK v NZ	Manchester	1999
2	318	Sourav Ganguly & Rahul Dravid	IND v SL	Taunton	1999
3	237*	Rahul Dravid & Schin Tendulkar	IND v KEN	Bristol	1999
4	204	Michael Clarke & Brad Hodge	AUS v HOL	Basseterre	2007
5	148	Toger Twose & Chris Cairns	NZ v AUS	Cardiff	1999
6	161	Maurice Odumbe & Allpesh Vadher	KEN v SL	Southampton	1999
7	98	Ramnaresh Sarwan & Ridley Jacobs	WI v NZ	Port Elizabeth	2003
8	117	David Houghton & Iain Butchart	ZIM v NZ	Hyderabad	1987
9	126*	Kapil Dev & Syed Kirmani	IND v ZIM	Tunbridge Wells	1983
10	71	Andy Roberts & Joel Garner	WI v IND	Manchester	1983

Top 10 batting strike rate

Strike Rate	Players	Match played	Highest	100s	50s	Average
121.17	Lance Klusener (SA)	14	57	-	3	124.00
115.84	John Davison(Canada)	9	111	1	2	34.11
115.15	Kapil Dev (IND)	29	175*	1	1	37.16
100.81	A De Villiers (SA)	10	146	1	2	37.20
100.70	Wasim Akram(PAK	38	43	-	-	19.36
98.01	Adam Gilchrist(AUS)	31	149	1	8	36.16
95.66	Virender Sehwag(IND)	14	114	1	2	33.07
94.98	Michael Clarke(AUS)	11	93*	-	4	87.20
94.71	Yuvraj Singh(IND)	14	83	-	3	37.20
94.07	Mark Boucher(SA)	25	75*	-	2	27.21

Leading top10-scrorers

Top Runs	Player	Country	Match played	HS	100	50
1796	Sachin Tendulkar	IND	36	152	4	13
1537	Ricky Ponting	AUS	39	140	4	6
1225	Brian Lara	WI	34	116	2	7
1165	Sanath Jaysuriya	SL	38	120	3	6
1085	Adam Gilchrist	AUS	31	149	1	8
1083	Javed Miandad	PAK	33	103	1	8
1075	Stephen Fleming	NZ	33	134	2	5
1067	Herschelle Gibbs	SA	25	143	2	8
1064	Aravinda de Silva	SL	35	145	2	6
1013	Vivian Richards	WI	23	181	3	5

BOWLING

Top 10-leading Wicket-takers

Bowler	Country	Wkts	Best
Glenn McGrath	AUS	53	4 for 19
Wasim Akram	PAK	49	6 for 25
Muttiah Murlitharan	SL	44	4 for 30
Chaminda Vass	SL	38	4 for 17
Javagal Srinath	IND	34	4 for 27
Allan Donald	SA	34	4 for 37
Brad Hogg	AUS	32	4 for 29
Imran Khan	PAK	32	4 for 07
Shane Warne	AUS	31	4 for 32
Chris Harris	NZ	31	5 for 36

Best bowlers' average

Bowler	Wkts for runs	Match	Place	Year
Glenn McGrath	7 for 15	AUS v NAM	Potchefstroom	2003
Andy Bichel	7 for 20	AUS v ENG	Port Elizabeth	2003
Winston Davis	7 for 51	WI v AUS	Leeds	1983
Gary Gilmour	6 for 14	AUS v ENG	Leeds	1975
Ashish Nehra	6 for 23	IND v ENG	Durban	2003
Shane Bond	6 for 23	NZ v AUS	Port Elizabeth	2003
Chaminda Vaas	6 for 25	SL v BAN-GLADESH	Pietermaritz-burg	2003
Ken Macleay	6 for 39	AUS v IND	Nottingham	1983

Best debut bowler and above 4 wkts +

Year	Bowler	Wkts for runs	Match
1975	Bernard Julien	4 for 20	WI v SL
1975	Dennis Lillee	5 for 34	AUS v PAK
1975	Gary Gilmour	6 for 14	AUS v ENG
1979	Michael Holding	4 for 33	WI v IND
1983	Duncan Fletcher	4 for 42	ZIM v AUS
1983	Abdul Qadir	4 for 21	PAK v NZ
1983	Winston Davis	7 for 51	WI v AUS
1987	Craig McDermott	4 for 56	AUS v IND
1996	Paul Strang	4 for 40	ZIM v WI
1996	Damien Fleming	5 for 36	AUS v IND
1999	Allan Mullally	4 for 37	ENG v SL
1999	Neil Johnson	4 for 42	ZIM v KENYA
1999	Debashish Mohanty	4 for 56	IND v KENYA
2003	Ian Harvey	4 for 58	AUS v PAK
2003	Austin Codrington	5 for 27	CAN v BANG
2003	Ian Harvey	4 for 58	AUS v PAK
2007	Farveez Maharoof	4 for 23	SL v BERMUDA

Wickets on 1st delivery

Bowler	Match	Place -	Year
Mark Ealham	ENG v SL	Lord's	1999
Ian Harvey	AUS v PAK	Johannesberg	2003
Mohammad Yousuf	PAK v ZIM	Kingston	2007

World Cup HAT TRICK

Bowler	Match	Place	Year
Chetan Sharma	IND v NZ	Nagpur	1987
Saqlain Mushtaq	PAK v ZIM	The Oval	1999
Chaminda Vass	SL v BANG	Pietermaritzburg	2003
Brett Lee	AUS v KENYA	Durban	2003
Lasith Malinga	SL v SA	Providence	2007

Most 05 expensive bowlers

Bowler	Run Rate	Over	Mdn	Runs	Wkt	Match	Place	Year
Devon Smith	11.20	5	0	56	2	WI v SA	St. Geroge's	2007
Rajab Ali	11.16	6	0	67	0	KEN v SL	Kanady	1996
Mark Gil-lespie	11.16	6	0	67	0	NZ v AUS	St. Geroge's	2007
Andre Adams	10.80	5	0	54	1	NZ v ZIM	Bloem-fontein	2003
Malachi Jones	10.57	7	0	74	1	BER v IND	Port of Spain	2007

Most 10 economical bowlers

Bowler	Run Rate	Over	Mdn	Run	Wkt	Match	Place	Year
Dermot Reeve	0.40	5	3	2	1	ENG v PAK	Adelaide	1992
Bishan Singh Bedi	0.50	12	8	8	1	IND v EAST AFR	Leeds	1975
Andre Botha	0.62	8	4	5	2	IRELAND v PAK	Kingston	2007
Mike Hendrick	0.62	8	4	5	1	ENG v CAN	Manchester	1979
Shaun Pollock	0.66	6	3	4	1	SA v HOLLAND	Basseterre	2007
Barry Wood	0.80	5	2	4	0	ENG v IND	Lord's	1975
Chris Old	0.80	10	5	8	4	ENG v CAN	Manchester	1979
Curtly Ambrose	0.80	10	4	8	2	WI v SCOTLAND	Leicester	1999
Richard Hadlee	0.83	12	6	10	0	NZ v EAST AFR	Brimingham	1975
Asif Khan	0.84	8.2	6	7	3	KENYA v AUS	Durban	2003

Best 10 all-round players

Player	Runs scored	Wkt tkn	Match	Place	Year
Keith Boyce	34	4 for 50	WI v AUS	Lord's	1975
Majid Khan	61	3 for 53	PAK v AUS	Nottingham	1979
Vivian Richards	42	3 for 52	WI v PAK	The Oval	1979
Duncan Fletcher	69*	4 for 42	ZIM v AUS	Nottingham	1983
Abdul Qadir	41*	4 for 21	PAK v NZ	Birmingham	1983
Jeremy Coney	33	3 for 28	NZ v PAK	Birmingham	1983
Kapil Dev	40	5 for 43	IND v AUS	Nottingham	1983
Richard Hadlee	31	3 for 32	NZ v ENG	Birmingham	1983
Kevin Curran	73	3 for 65	ZIM v IND	Tunbridge wells	1983
Mohd. Azharuddin	54*	3 for 19	IND v AUS	New Delhi	1987

Best team record

Country	No.of match	Won	Lost	NO result	Winning rate
AUS	69	51	17	1	74.66
SA	40	25	13	2	65.00
WI	57	35	21	1	62.28
ENG	59	36	22	1	61.86
NZ	62	35	26	1	57.22
IND	58	32	25	1	56.03
PAK	56	30	24	2	55.35
SL	57	25	30	2	45.61
KENYA	23	6	16	1	28.26
IRELAND	9	2	6	1	27.77
BANG	20	5	14	1	27.50
ZIM	45	8	33	4	22.22
UAE	5	1	4	0	20.00
HOLLAND	14	2	12	0	14.28
CANADA	12	1	11	0	8.33
EAST AFR	3	0	3	0	0
BERMUDA	3	0	3	0	0
NAMBIA	6	0	6	0	0
SCOTLAND	8	0	8	0	0

Year-wise batting pattern

Year	Total Match	First	Second (chasing)	No Result
1975	15	8	7	0
1979	14	7	7	0
1983	27	15	12	0
1987	27	19	8	0
1992	39	18	19	2
1996	36	17	18	1
1999	42	19	21	2
2003	52	29	20	3
2007	51	25	25	1
Total	303	157	137	9

Top 05 wicket-keeping batsman

Player	Country	No.of Match	Runs	Str.Rt	Stumping	Catch	Average
Adam Gilchrist	AUS	31	1085	98.01	7	45	36.16
K.Sangakkara	SL	21	526	74.71	6	26	30.94
Mark Boucher	SA	25	381	94.07	0	31	27.21
Moin Khan	PAK	20	286	106.31	7	23	28.60
Alec Stewart	ENG	20	520	66.49	2	21	32.50

Top 5 highest total score

Final Score	Match	Country	Place	Year
413 for 5	IND v BER-MUDA	IND	Port of Spain	2007
398 for 5	SL v KENYA	SL	Kandy	1996
377 for 6	AUS v SA	AUS	Basseterre	2007
373 for 6	IND v SL	IND	Taunton	1999
363 for 5	NZ v CANADA	NZ	Gross Islet	2007

Top 5 lowest total score

Final Score	Match	Country	Place	Year
104	KEN v WI	KEN	Kimberley	2003
108	BANG v SA	BANG	Bloemfotein	2003
112	NZ v AUS	NZ	Port Elizabeth	2003
122	HOL v AUS	HOL	Potchefstroom	2003
125	IND v AUS	IND	Centurion	2003

Highest total in Finals

Final Score	Match	Place	Year
359 for 2	AUS v IND	Johannesburg	2003

Lowest total in Finals

Final Score	Match	Place	Year
132	PAK v AUS	Lord's	1999